GCSE Food Technology for OCR

Second edition

Jenny Ridgwell

RECOGNISING ACHIEVEMENT

Heinemann Educational Publishers
Halley Court, Jordan Hill, Oxford OX2 8EJ
a division of Reed Educational and Professional
Publishing Ltd.
Heinemann is a registered trademark of Reed
Educational and Professional Publishing Ltd.

OXFORD MELBOURNE AUCKLAND
KAMPALA JOHANNESBURG BLANTYRE GABORONE
IBADAN PORTSMOUTH (NH) USA CHICAGO

Text © Jenny Ridgwell, 1999, 2001

First published 1999
This edition 2001

05 04 03 02 01
10 9 8 7 6 5 4 3 2

British Library Cataloguing in Publication Data
A catalogue record for this book is available from the
British Library

ISBN 0 435 41951 X

Designed and typeset by Artistix, Thame, Oxon
Illustrations by Diana Bowles
Cover image by Tokay
Printed and bound in Great Britain by Bath
Colourbooks, Glasgow

Acknowledgements

The author and publisher would like to thank Barbara
Di Nicoli for updating the coursework section and The
Dronfield School and The Lady Eleanor Holles School, in
particular Elenis Josephides for the examples of shown work
on pp. 148–156.

The publisher would like to thank the following for
permission to reproduce copyright material.
Birds Eye Wall's for the chart on p. 91; British Nutrition
Foundation for the material on p. 36, adapted from original
material developed by the British Nutrition Foundation;
British Soft Drinks for the chart on p. 80, reproduced
courtesy of the British Soft Drinks Association; Campden and
Chorleywood Food Research Association for the materials on
pp. 8, 22; Cereal Partners UK for the packaging on p. 98;
Daily Mail/Solo Syndication for the extracts on pp. 34, 57;
Design and Technology Association (DATA) for the adapted
version of text from *Food Technology in Practice* on
pp. 122–23; Design in Action for the interview on p. 98;
Economatics (Education) Ltd for the material on p. 87; H.J.
Heinz Co. Ltd for the label from Heinz's 'Barbie Pasta Shapes
in Tomato Sauce' on p. 17; Health Education Authority for
the material from *Scientific Basis for Dental Health Education*,
1996, on p. 55 and 'The Balance of Good Health Wheel',

reproduced with permission on p. 15; Hill & Knowlton for
the label from Bestfood Ltd 'Ambrosia Devon Custard' on
p. 63 and the material on Quorn™ on p. 21; The Stationery
Office for the data from *Composition of Foods*, by McCance
and Widdowson, on p. 73 and the data from the *Report on
Health and Social Subjects 41* on p. 14: Crown copyright
material is reproduced with the permission of the Controller
of Her Majesty's Stationery Office; MAFF for the cover of
About food additives (PB1552) on p. 62, reproduced by
permission of MAFF. © Crown copyright; Manor Bakeries for
the material on p. 65; Marks and Spencer for the packaging
on p. 53 and the 'Healthier choice' symbols on
p. 11; McDonald's Restaurants Ltd for the data from *Food
2000* on p. 27; Meat and Livestock Commission for the
material taken from 'The Meat in Your Sandwich' video-based
learning pack, on p. 90; Multivac for the diagram on p. 70;
New Covent Garden Soup Company for the material on
pp. 110–111; Newton House Bakery for the packaging from
'Smiley Face Cakes' on p. 55; Noon Products Ltd for the
material on pp. 88, 116–17; Nutricia for the material on
p. 143; Patak (Spices) Limited for the material on pp. 17, 92–95;
Ridgwell Press for the material on pp. 103–107; Sainsbury's
Supermarkets Ltd for the material on pp. 11, 15, 18, 22, 48,
49, 74, 101, 103; Sally Hookham, p. 76; Science Photo Library
for the picture on p. 13; Tesco Stores for the screen from
their CD-ROM on p. 133; The Telegraph/Ewan McNaughton
Associates for the headline on p. 31; The Yorkshire Post for
the headlines on p. 31; VSUK Trading Limited for the
Vegetarian Society Trademark on p. 20.

The publishers would like to thank the following for
permission to use photographs:
Ace photos, p. 95; Alexis Maryon, p. 28; APV Baker, p. 88 (all);
Cabinplant, p. 67 (bottom); Campden and Chorleywood,
p. 78; Chris Honeywell, pp. 112–13 (all); Comas, pp. 120–21
(all), 122 (middle right); Cortecs Diagnostics Ltd, p. 19
(bottom); Crosse and Blackwell, p. 9; Danesco, pp. 97, 99;
ETI, pp. 25 (top), 32 (both); FAM, p. 67 (top right);
Federation of Bakers, p. 81 (all); Food Features, pp. 39
(middle), 56 (all), 144; Food Safe, p. 25 (bottom); Gareth
Boden, pp. 35, 39 (bottom), 44, 45, 46, 47, 51 (all), 54, 60
(all), 69, 96 (all), 122 (top left); Ian Berry/Magnum,
pp. 114–15 (all); Jenny Ridgwell, pp. 75, 118, 138 (all);
Lakeland Ltd, pp. 66 (all), 67 (top two, left), 129; Manchester
Airport, p. 34; Manor Bakeries, p. 65 (both); Meg Sullivan,
pp. 26, 88; NATHE, p. 77; National Dairy Council, p. 50;
New Covent Garden Soup Company, p. 111; Noon Products
Ltd, p. 116; Nutricia Dietary Products, p. 19 (top); Otto
Kremmling, pp. 122 (top and bottom, right), 123; Rank Hovis,
pp. 39, 40, 85 (both); Sainsbury Supermarkets Ltd, p. 33
(both); Value Food Brokers, p. 53.

The publisher would like to thank Tokay for permission to
reproduce the cover image.

Contents

Introduction

This book has been updated to meet the specification requirements for the OCR GCSE in Design and Technology: Food Technology. The book covers all the requirements for the Short Course. If you are following the full course, some extra material is provided in the Teacher's Resource File. The OCR specification is designed to meet the National Curriculum Orders for Design and Technology and the GCSE Subject Criteria for Design and Technology.

The programme of study for Design and Technology at Key Stage 4 requires you to develop your Design and Technology capability by applying knowledge and understanding when developing ideas, planning, making products and evaluating them.

The OCR specification content provides opportunities for you to develop Design and Technology capability through activities, including:

- product analysis
- focused practical tasks, that develop a range of techniques, skills, processes and knowledge.
- design and make assignments, which include activities related to industrial practices and the application of **systems** and control.

You will be assessed in two ways. You will have to do internal assessment (coursework) (for up to 60% of the marks). You will also have to do a written examination at the end of the course (for up to 40% of the marks).

How to use the book

The book is divided into the following sections:
- Nutritional needs and food choices
- Hygiene and safety
- Food ingredients
- Food production
- Industrial case studies
- Food Technology skills.

This book can be used to help you:
- develop your food technology skills
- develop your knowledge and understanding of food technology, specifically for the content requirements of the OCR specification
- understand what is required for internal assessment (coursework)
- develop the key skills of communication, application of number, information technology, working with others, problem solving and improving own learning through your food technology work.

The book is written in a series of double-page spreads. Each double-page spread includes:
- specification links – these show which sections of the specification are covered by the double-page spread.
- questions – these test knowledge and understanding, and can be used in independent study and for revision
- key points – these give you a summary of what is on the spread and will be useful for revision.

Symbols are used on the spreads to show work covering ICT and industrial practice:

indicates ICT

 indicates industrial practice.

 At the end of each section there is a set of more detailed questions which relate to the topics covered in the section as a whole.

This book is supported by a Teacher's Resource File, which provides more information on certain topics, proformas for coursework, and extra material for the Full Course. When extra material is provided in the Teacher's Resource File this is shown by the symbol:
Your teacher will let you have the sheets you need.

Food Technology is an ever-changing subject and, as a result, many types of resource are required to provide research and up-to-date information. The Internet is a valuable support in searching for help, and some useful website addresses have been provided on page 143. Much of the research for this book was carried out through the Internet.

Notes for teachers

The OCR GCSE in Design and Technology: Food Technology specification allows candidates to acquire and apply knowledge, skills and understanding through:

- analysing and evaluating products and processes
- engaging in focussed tasks to develop and demonstrate techniques
- engaging in strategies for developing ideas, planning and producing products
- considering how past and present design and technology, relevant to a designing and making context, affects society
- recognising the moral, cultural and environmental issues inherent in design and technology.

Assessment objectives

Within this specification candidates will need to demonstrate their ability to:

- develop, plan and communicate ideas
- work with tools, equipment, materials and components to produce quality products
- evaluate processes and products
- understand materials and components
- understand systems and control.

The GCSE Subject Criteria (QCA 2000) sets out three specification Assessment Objectives for the scheme of assessment:

AO1 Capability through acquiring and applying knowledge, skills and understanding of materials components, processes, techniques and industrial practice

AO2 Capability through acquiring and applying knowledge, skills and understanding when designing and making quality products

AO3 Capability through acquiring and applying knowledge, skills and understanding when evaluating processes and products; and examining the wider effects of design and technology on society.

Examination

The terminal examination papers will test candidates' specialist knowledge/skills and understanding of Food Technology through questions on the subject content outlined in the specification.

Internal assessment (coursework)

The specification assesses QCA's three assessment objectives in an integrated way through the following six internal assessment objectives:

- identify a need or opportunity that leads to a design brief
- conduct research into the design brief which results in a specification
- generate possible ideas for a solution
- develop the product for manufacture
- plan and realize the product
- evaluate and test the product.

Acknowledgements

The book has been developed with the support of OCR. A special thank you goes to Barbara Di Nicoli, the Chief Examiner for Food Technology for providing information and for checking the text. Examples of students' work from The Dronfield School and The Lady Eleanor Holles School have been used in the book.

Further information

The range of knowledge and information required for Food Technology GCSE cannot be covered adequately in one book. A list of other useful resources is provided on page 157.

Enjoy the work.

Jenny Ridgwell, 2001

NUTRITIONAL NEEDS AND FOOD CHOICES

Food product development

5.1.1b, c, 5.2.1i

The OCR GCSE in Food Technology focuses on developing marketable food products. To do this you need to know about the food industry, and how new products are developed and launched.

In 1999 in the UK 7500 new food and drink products were developed for sale in supermarkets. You can see from the chart that the number of new food products is increasing nearly every year.

New food and drink products

Year	Number	% growth
1990	2933	
1991	3233	10.2
1992	3823	18.2
1993	4525	18.4
1994	4815	6.4
1995	4596	−4.5
1996	4614	0.4
1997	6159	33.5
1998	7600	23
1999	7500	−1.3

Source: *Product Intelligence Notes*, Campden and Chorleywood Food Research Association

Food trends

These are some of the food **trends** in the past few years:

- the number of new food products and the range of foods is increasing
- there is an increase in the development of authentic ethnic foods such as noodle and rice dishes
- more and more sandwiches are being eaten
- there is an increase in traditional food products such as bread and butter pudding
- the amount of foods with healthy eating claims, especially low-fat or no-fat claims, is increasing
- the variety of vegetable dishes is increasing
- more new products targeted at children – 349 in 1997
- there is an increase in organic foods and products suitable for vegetarians
- party food is proving popular
- many people have microwave ovens so microwavable foods are increasing.

These trends show that our attitude to eating ready-prepared foods is changing. People seem to be choosing to buy more foods that are ready to eat or just need reheating. As we travel more around the world and learn about food from other cultures we want to try these dishes for ourselves.

People are spending less time in the kitchen preparing foods from raw ingredients and there is also an increase in the trend to eat away from home. In some homes, some of the traditional mealtimes of breakfast, lunch and dinner are being replaced by snack meals and by take-away meals. There is also an increase in the number of people living on their own in the UK.

Our food choices are increasing rapidly, and the technology in the food industry supports the development of different ways to produce and package new products. The food industry is also developing a range of modern and smart materials which will affect the way food products are made.

Trends of the future?

These predictions about future food trends are from research done by CCFRA (Campden and Chorleywood Food Research Association):

- more variety of choice and convenience
- more demand for healthier foods and organic ingredients
- greater demand for single **portions**
- more products that can be microwaved
- new food products will look and taste more 'home made'.

New product launch

A new range of frozen ready-meals is on the market. New York Take Out is a New York style noodle take-away in a carton with its own menu number on the side for that real take-away feel! Just microwave for 10 minutes from frozen, stirring once half-way, and you can eat the NYTO from the box.

Many new food products are being developed

Keys to success

To succeed a new product needs:

- thorough market research
- to make good use of the technology of manufacturing
- plenty of testing with consumers
- plenty of advertising through TV and the press.

People constantly want new products but there is still a need for basic products. These are products that are very familiar, widely available and with low profit margins such as baked beans and sliced bread. New products that provide something different are often called **added value** products. They are usually new, attractive, convenient to use and exciting.

Questions

1 Explain in your own words why you think we are buying more ready-prepared foods. Describe three different reasons in your answer.

2 Draw a graph to show the changes in the number of new food and drink products launched in the UK from 1990 to 1999.

3 Why do you think people want foods that are a) healthier, b) organic, c) single portions? Give an example of each of these foods.

4 Give your views on the New York Take Out. What is the **target group** for this product? Why does it have a modern appeal? How might this product develop into other recipes?

Key points

- Lifestyles and technology are changing our food choices.
- The development of new food products is increasing.

Food choices

Food provides us with nutrients to keep us alive and healthy. Eating is enjoyable and mealtimes are an occasion to share with friends and family. We need to eat a variety of foods for a healthy balanced **diet.** The nutrients we need are:

- proteins, which are body building and help with growth and repair
- carbohydrates and fats, which supply the body with energy
- vitamins and minerals, which are protective and help to keep us healthy.

Energy from food

The energy value from food comes from its fat, protein and carbohydrate content. Fat provides almost twice as much energy as the same weight of carbohydrate or protein. Energy is measured in kilojoules (kJ) and kilocalories (kcal).

Energy produced by nutrients

	kcal per g	kJ per g
Protein	4	17
Carbohydrate	3.75	16
Fat	9	38

Protein is needed for growth and repair of body tissues, muscles and blood cells. People in the UK are unlikely to suffer from lack of protein. Foods that supply protein include meat, fish, poultry, eggs and milk. Vegetable sources include peas, beans and cereals.

Fats supply a concentrated source of energy. Fat should not supply more than 35% of our food energy according to the COMA report 1991. Foods that are high in fat include those fried in oil or fat, such as fried fish and chips.

There are two types of carbohydrate – starch and sugar. Carbohydrates are mainly used to provide energy. We should increase the amount of starchy, NSP-(dietary fibre)-rich foods that we eat. Foods that provide carbohydrate include bread, pasta, rice and breakfast cereals.

Vitamins and minerals

Vitamins and minerals are called **micronutrients** since they are needed in smaller quantities than the **macronutrients** – protein, carbohydrate and fat. Water-soluble vitamins include vitamin C and the B group vitamins, and foods rich in these vitamins should be eaten regularly. Fat-soluble vitamins include vitamins A, D, E and K. Vitamins C, E and beta-carotene are called the anti-oxidant vitamins and a diet rich in these vitamins is thought to reduce the risk of heart disease and cancer. Vitamin C is found in fruits and vegetables. Oranges and lemons are good sources of vitamin C.

The two minerals most often lacking in the diet are calcium and iron. Calcium is needed for strong bones and teeth, and iron is needed to form part of the haemoglobin which gives red blood cells their colour. A deficiency of iron can lead to anaemia.

Sodium is needed to control body fluids. The most common form of sodium in our diet is salt. We are advised to reduce our daily salt intake to 6 grams a day.

Dietary fibre

Dietary fibre is called non-starch polysaccharide (NSP) and is needed for the digestive system to function properly and to prevent constipation. We are advised to increase the amount of NSP (dietary fibre) by eating more wholegrain foods, fruits, vegetables, pulses and nuts.

Note: On food labels and in food claims, NSP (dietary fibre) is called fibre. In this book, the term NSP will be used in nutrition information and the term fibre on food labels.

The nutrients on food labels

Food labels provide you with plenty of information about the nutritional value of the food product.

NUTRITION INFORMATION		
TYPICAL VALUES (COOKED AS PER INSTRUCTIONS)		
	PER ½ PACK	PER 100g
ENERGY	1138 k J.	481 k J.
	296 k cal	115 k cal
PROTEIN	20.1g	7.9g
CARBOHYDRATE	28.3g	11.1g
of which sugars	7.4g	2.9g
of which starch	20.9g	8.2g
FAT	19.4g	7.6g
of which saturates	7.7g	3.0g
of which mono-unsaturates	9.1g	3.2g
FIBRE	less than 0.1g	less than 0.1g
SODIUM	less than 0.1g	less than 0.1g
PER ½ PACK	296 CAL	19.4g FAT
GUIDELINE DAILY AMOUNTS		
EACH DAY	WOMEN	MEN
CALORIES	2000 k cal	2500 k cal
FAT	70g	95g
RECOMMENDED BY NUTRITION PROFESSIONALS FOR AVERAGE ADULTS		

A typical food label

- Energy – the amount of energy provided in a food is shown as kcal and kJ.
- Carbohydrate – this is the total amount of carbohydrate in the food. It is made up of two forms: starch and sugars. 'Of which sugars' shows how much of the total carbohydrate comes from sugars. Sometimes the amount of starch is also shown.
- Fat – this is the total amount of fat in the food. This includes saturates, polyunsaturates and mono-unsaturates, which are the different types of fat found in food. Current advice is that the average amount of saturates eaten should be reduced. The suggested average is 20 grams of saturates a day for women of normal weight, and 30 grams for men.
- Sodium is a mineral found naturally in most foods but also added during manufacture, mostly as salt.
- Vitamins and minerals – these are only shown on the label if the food contains at least 15% of the RDA (Recommended Daily Allowance).

Many foods are designed to meet specific nutritional needs. Food companies may use symbols to identify nutritional claims such as high-fibre, low fat and reduced fat.

Symbols used by Marks & Spencer

Factors affecting food choice

- Availability – in the UK most food is sold through supermarkets and is supplied from around the world. Food is no longer just available when it is in season in the UK. Strawberries can be bought throughout the year. However, fruits and vegetables should be cheaper when they are in season.
- Cost – people often choose to eat what they can afford to buy. Many families have to budget carefully to buy the food they need. They look for products that are good value for money. This can change from week to week depending upon seasonal changes and supermarket offers.
- Lifestyle – people's lifestyle often affects where and when they eat. People who work in the evening or take part in activities such as sport may choose to have their main meal at lunchtime and eat a snack in the evening.
- Storage – people may not have the space to store large quantities of food. For example, students living in student accommodation may share a kitchen with several other students and they buy small quantities of food and shop regularly for ingredients for cooking.

Questions

1 List the macronutrients and describe their function in our diet.

2 List some of the micronutrients and describe the function of three of them.

3 How would you encourage people to eat more NSP (dietary fibre)?

4 Why is the nutritional information on a food label useful? Give three reasons.

Key points

- Food is made up of a variety of nutrients.
- Food labels provide information on the nutritional value of the product.
- Prices of fruits and vegetables come down when they are in season locally.

Food issues

5.1.11c, 5.2.1g, i, 5.2.5f

Reducing chemicals and waste

Food processing factories and packaging companies need to be aware of the environmental issues involved in the processes they use. It is important to reduce the use of toxic chemicals which are dangerous to the environment including bleaches, CFCs and toxic metals. Factories, shops and businesses all have a duty to dispose of waste products safely.

Chlorofluorocarbon (CFC) is one of the chemicals released into the atmosphere through the use of refrigerators and aerosols and it is considered to be harmful to the ozone layer.

Modern food materials

Modern food materials can include modified enzymes, starches, antioxidants, genetically engineered foods and synthetic flavours which are used to provide certain properties in food products.

Modified enzymes

These have be changed by chemical modification or genetic modification. In some types of cheesemaking, a genetically modified enzyme is used. The genetic information for the chymosin enzyme in calf rennet has been identified and copied into yeast cells. These yeast cells produce pure chymosin, which is the same as the animal enzyme, but is made by a yeast cell which is not of animal origin.

Modified starch

There are many types of **modified starch**. Each one has a different function depending on the way the starch has been modified. In instant desserts, the starch is added in a pre-gelatinised form which swells in cold water, thickening the product without the use of heat. In canned soups, the starch is bonded with phosphate which allows the starch to absorb more water and helps to keep the ingredients in the soup together. In French dressing, the hydrophobic part of the starch wraps around the oil droplet, so the hydrophilic part of the starch is in contact with the water. This keeps the oil droplets suspended in the water.

In jelly beans, starch is treated with an acid to produce a very strong gel which forms the shell of the jelly bean. If the starch is oxidized, this improves its binding properties, which can be used to increase the stickiness of foods such as the batter applied to fish.

(Information on modified starch taken from information published by the British Nutrition Foundation on Modified Starch.)

Smart foods

Smart materials respond to differences in temperature or light and change in some way. They are called 'smart' because they sense conditions in their environment and respond to them. Smart or modern foods are developed through new or improved processes. They are altered to perform a particular function. An example is modified starches, where the starch has been chemically modified or processed. Modified starches respond to differences in temperatures. For example, these particular starches thicken in hot water or when heated, but return to a flow when cool. Some pizza toppings use modified starch which has been treated with a chlorine solution. The topping thickens when heated in the oven and will not run off the pizza. On cooling, the topping becomes runny.

(All information for this section is from Design and Technology National Curriculum for England and also supplied by QCA.)

Anti-oxidants

These prolong shelf life, stop fatty food from going rancid and protect fat-soluble vitamins from combining with oxygen. Anti-oxidants are used in dried soups, cheese spreads and sausages.

Genetic modification/engineering

Genetic modification or genetic engineering can be used to change the characteristics of some food ingredients. Scientists can identify and modify or engineer a gene that makes up a characteristic in a food. Genetic material can be transferred between plants, animals and micro-organisms to control flavour, nutritional content and qualities during processing and cooking. The first genetically modified or engineered food on sale in the UK was tomato paste, made from tomatoes that ripen slowly, allowing them to be left longer before picking without going soft. New varieties of crops have been developed and the genetic modification or engineering helps to improve the crops' resistance to pests and diseases. These crops are grown on a commercial scale in the USA and experimental trials have been carried out in the UK. Crop protection can reduce the use of pesticides.

There are concerns for the environmental effects of growing these crops, and some groups of people are anxious about the possible cross pollination from one species to another. There has been much debate on TV and in newspapers about the safety of using this technology. In the UK, all food must be fit for human consumption as required by the Food Safety Act. Several committees assess the safety and controls for genetic modification or engineering, including the Advisory Committee on Novel Foods and Processes (ACNFP).

Synthetic flavours

These are also called artificial flavours. They are made from chemicals and provide a flavour which is similar, but not identical, to a natural or nature-identical flavour.

BSE

Bovine Spongiform Encephalopathy (BSE), sometimes known as 'mad cow' disease, is a disease which affects the nervous system of cattle and was identified in 1986. BSE is a progressive degenerative disease which causes microscopic holes in the brains of affected animals.

The animals become uncoordinated, nervous and eventually die. BSE is believed to be caused by contaminated animal feed. It is thought that cows were infected from the feed which contained the processed sheep's brains infected with scrapie. The outbreak reached its peak in Britain early in 1993, and since then the number of cases has declined. The government has introduced procedures to protect animal health, and in time hopes to eradicate BSE. In 1988 a feed ban was introduced to prevent infectious material being used in animal feedstuff. In 1997, animals which might have been exposed to infection were slaughtered and this led to a decline in the incidence of BSE. Sales of British beef have been affected, as some people choose not to eat beef.

CJD (Creutzfeldt-Jakob Disease) is the human equivalent of BSE and deaths from CJD have recently begun to increase.

A cow suffering from BSE

Questions

1 Explain the following terms in your own words: modified enzymes; modified starch; smart foods; genetic modification or engineering.

2 Explain what is meant by BSE and CJD.

3 Through scientific research food information is constantly changing – keep up-to-date with research through the Food Standards website (www.foodstandards.gov.uk).

Dietary goals

There are several campaigns to help us improve our eating habits and lifestyles. Here are some of them.

Saving lives – our healthier nation 1999

This government white paper sets targets to reduce the death rate for cancer, coronary heart disease and strokes by a variety of means including improving the national diet.

COMA

The Committee on Medical Aspects of Food Policy (COMA) produced a report in 1991 called *Dietary Reference Values for Food Energy and Nutrients for the UK* which set **Dietary Reference Values (DRVs)** to show the amount of food energy or other nutrients needed by people of different ages. The aim of the COMA report is to make sure that everyone gets enough of each nutrient to meet their needs.

COMA daily dietary recommendations for energy and nutrients

Nutrient	Dietary recommendations Reference Nutrient Intake (RNI) per day
Energy value of food	varies with age, sex and activity adult male 2550 kcal adult female 1940 kcal
Protein	55 g for men, 45 g for women
Fat	no more than 35% of food energy
Carbohydrates of which starch	50% of energy value of food 39% of energy value
sugars (NME – non-milk extrinsic sugars)	11% of energy value
NSP (dietary fibre)	18 g for adults
Vitamins	based on individual needs
Minerals	based on individual needs

- **Reference Nutrient Intake (RNI)** is the amount of nutrient sufficient for nearly everyone (about 97% of the population), even those with high needs. This level of intake is considered to be higher than most people need.

- **Estimated Average Requirement (EAR)** is the amount of the average need for food energy or a nutrient. The EAR is not the recommended intake for an individual but is the estimate of the average need for a large group of people. Some people will need more, some people will need less.

- **Lower reference nutrient intake (LRNI)** is the amount of nutrient that is enough for only a small number of people who have low needs.

Dietary recommendations for fat

The COMA report of 1991 recommended that no more than 35% of our energy should come from fat in food. The national average is about 41% of energy from fat, so many people need to cut down on the amount of fatty foods they eat.

Dietary recommendations for carbohydrates

The COMA report suggested that we should increase the amount of foods rich in starch and NSP (dietary fibre) but reduce the sugary foods in our diet.

Dietary recommendations for sugar

The COMA report suggested that we should cut down the amount of sugar that we eat, to 11% of energy intake. These sugars are called non-milk extrinsic sugars (NMEs). This type of sugar is found in table sugar, sweets, sugary drinks, cakes and biscuits and is added to many processed foods.

The Dietary Reference Value for non-milk extrinsic sugars is 60 grams per day.

Dietary recommendations for salt

The COMA report on cardiovascular disease published in 1994 recommended that people of all ages should cut down on their salt intake. The average intake of salt in the UK is 9 grams. The advice is to reduce this to 6 grams a day.

Recommendations for NSP (dietary fibre)

In COMA's recommendations the Dietary Reference Value (DRV) for NSP (dietary fibre) is 18 grams.

Dietary changes	Tips for making these changes
Reduce the amount of fat	Reduce the quantity of fat used in cooking, choose lower-fat versions of food ingredients, remove visible fat from meat, bacon and poultry.
Reduce the amount of sugar	Reduce the amount of sugar used in recipes, avoid eating foods that contain large amounts of sugar.
Reduce the amount of salt	Add less salt to recipes and avoid ingredients that contain a lot of sodium.
Increase the amount of NSP (dietary fibre)	Eat more wholegrain foods including bread and cereals, eat more fruit and vegetables, pulses and nuts.

The Balance of Good Health

In 1994, the National Food Guide, *The Balance of Good Health*, was published. It was based on the government's eight guidelines for a healthy diet (produced by the Ministry of Agriculture, Fisheries and Food). The key message of *The Balance of Good Health* is that a balance of foods should be consumed to achieve a good healthy diet. This balance should be achieved over a week or two and is not essential for every meal.

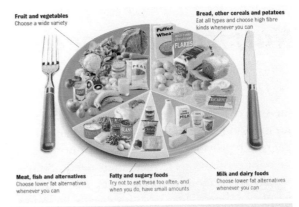

Fruit and vegetables
Choose a wide variety

Bread, other cereals and potatoes
Eat all types and choose high fibre kinds whenever you can

Meat, fish and alternatives
Choose lower fat alternatives whenever you can

Fatty and sugary foods
Try not to eat these too often, and when you do, have small amounts

Milk and dairy foods
Choose lower fat alternatives whenever you can

The foods that make up The Balance of Good Health

Meeting nutritional needs

Supermarkets help with food choices by labelling foods to show if they are low in sugar, fat and salt, or high in fibre. The Institute of Grocery Distribution has set guidelines, which are shown on some food labels. These guidelines are as follows:

Men		Women	
Calories	Fat	Calories	Fat
2500	95 g	2000	70 g

The Institute of Grocery Distribution guidelines

Questions

1 Write about the three main health campaigns for dietary goals described in this section.

2 Use the picture for The Balance of Good Health to describe how a balance of foods helps to make a healthy diet.

3 What is meant by the terms DRV, RNI and NME?

Key points

- There are several health campaigns to help improve habits and lifestyles in the UK.
- Dietary Reference Values provide guidelines on the amount of nutrients we need.

Nutritional needs

The type of food and drink that we eat is called our diet. Some people eat a healthy, balanced diet which provides all the necessary nutrients in the right proportions to meet their needs. Some people need to follow special diets. For example, people wanting to lose weight follow a slimming diet and people with coeliac disease choose a gluten-free diet.

People have different nutritional needs, and these needs change with age and with the level of physical activity a person does.

Babies

Experts recommend that babies should be breast fed for at least four months. When babies change from milk to solid food this is called weaning. Foods should be nutritious and mashed to a smooth texture so that the baby can eat it easily.

Children

Children need to eat a variety of foods to provide a range of nutrients and to help them explore a range of tastes and flavours. Their diets should include a range of starch, NSP-(dietary fibre)-rich foods such as wholemeal bread, beans and potatoes.

Small children need smaller portions of food than adults and should not eat too many sugary or fatty snacks as these can fill them up and they may not be hungry for more nutritious food.

Older children

Teenagers are growing fast and have higher energy needs than adults. They also have increased requirements for iron, calcium and all vitamins. Teenagers often 'graze' and eat snacks, so their foods should provide a range of nutrients to meet dietary needs.

Pregnancy

The diet before and during pregnancy can affect the success of the pregnancy and the health of the mother and baby. Energy and protein requirements increase slightly during pregnancy, and women are advised to make sure that their diet contains adequate supplies of folic acid, iron, calcium and vitamin D.

Older people

Older people tend to need less energy from foods as they are often less active than younger people. Their foods should supply a range of nutrients and they should follow the healthy eating guidelines.

Food products

Food products are designed to appeal to people of different ages. The food industry designs products to appeal to a target market, which is the range of people that the product is aimed at. Information on the target market can include the age range, sex, income, career and location. So the target market for a fruit yogurt could be young children, aged 5–10 years.

Image boards

When designers are working on product and packaging ideas they often create an **image board** to show ideas. An image board shows images of a theme or target group, using pictures, photos, graphs and drawings.

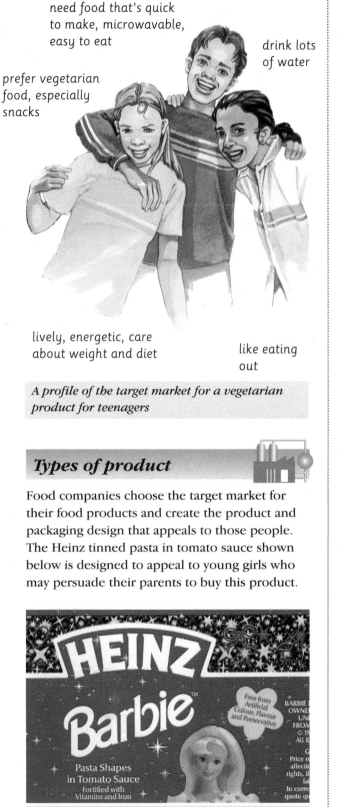

need food that's quick
to make, microwavable,
easy to eat

drink lots
of water

prefer vegetarian
food, especially
snacks

lively, energetic, care
about weight and diet

like eating
out

*A profile of the target market for a vegetarian
product for teenagers*

Types of product

Food companies choose the target market for
their food products and create the product and
packaging design that appeals to those people.
The Heinz tinned pasta in tomato sauce shown
below is designed to appeal to young girls who
may persuade their parents to buy this product.

*A product designed to appeal to a
particular market*

Questions

A DELICIOUS QUICK AND EASY
SNACK OR MEAL. PERFECT STUFF FOR THE KIDS!

1 What is the target group for this range of
Kids Stuff? Describe three new products
that you think would be suitable for this
range. Give reasons for your answers.

2 Create an image board to show pictures
associated with teenagers and/or
toddlers.

Key points

● People have different nutritional needs,
which change with age and activity.

● Food products are designed to appeal to
different people.

Food to meet special needs

p.34

5.2.1h, i, 5.2.3a

Diabetes

Diabetes mellitus is a condition in which the amount of glucose (sugar) in the blood is too high because the body is not able to convert glucose into energy. Nearly three-quarters of a million people in the UK are known to have diabetes, so it is a common health condition. People with diabetes do not need to eat a special diet. They can follow the dietary guidelines for healthy eating that are recommended for everyone. So their diet should be high in NSP (dietary fibre) and low in sugar and fat.

Food intolerance and allergy

True food intolerance affects less than 2% of the population. A food intolerance happens when the body reacts to certain food ingredients. The most common foods that cause reactions are egg, peanuts and other nuts, cow's milk, wheat, fish, shellfish, soya bean and rice. An allergy is a type of intolerance.

INGREDIENTS
POTATO SKINS: POTATO, VEGETABLE OIL, SALT, GARLIC, CHILLI, PEPPER, BLACK PEPPER, CUMIN, PAPRIKA, CELERY SEED, DEXTROSE, DEHYDRATED ONION, HERBS, HYDROGENATED VEGETABLE OIL
SOURED CREAM AND CHIVE DIP: SOURED CREAM, DRIED CHIVES, ONION, ONION SALT, STABILISER: XANTHAN GUM.
*CONTAINS MILK

Information on labels helps people with food intolerance or allergy

Coeliac disease (gluten intolerance)

People with coeliac disease are unable to eat products made from wheat, barley, oats and rye as they are sensitive to the protein gluten which is found in these cereals. The only way to control this disease is to eat a gluten-free diet.

Gluten-free products are widely available and they are clearly labelled with this symbol:

Gluten Free

Type of intolerance or allergy	Foods to be avoided	Symptoms	What to do
milk intolerance	cows' milk	wind, cramps, diarrhoea	use other milks or soya milk
gluten intolerance	wheat, rye, oats, barley food products	children don't grow properly, weight loss	use gluten-free foods
wheat intolerance	foods made from the whole of the wheat grain	asthma, itchy skin, diarrhoea	avoid all foods made from wheat
peanut allergy	foods made with peanuts	affects breathing, can cause anaphylactic shock	avoid all foods made with peanuts
egg allergy	food products made from eggs	eczema and rash	avoid all egg products
fish and shellfish allergy	all fish and shellfish	nettle rash and anaphylactic shock	avoid all fish and shellfish
soya allergy	soya products such as tofu, soy sauce	eczema, asthma and diarrhoea	avoid soya products
certain colourings and preservatives	food products made with certain colourings and preservatives	may cause hyperactivity in children	avoid food products made with certain colourings and preservatives

In a healthy person, the lining of the small intestine is covered in fingerlike villi, which increase the surface area to help food absorption. If someone with a coeliac condition eats gluten, the lining becomes inflamed and the villi flatten and food is not absorbed properly.

Glutafin is a range of gluten-free foods

Peanut and nut allergies

A whole range of foods can cause anaphylaxis. Peanuts and other nuts are the most common trigger. Anaphylactic shock is a very serious, potentially fatal condition and can develop in sensitive people within a few seconds or minutes of eating peanuts.

The food industry uses a peanut-testing kit to identify the presence of peanuts in products.

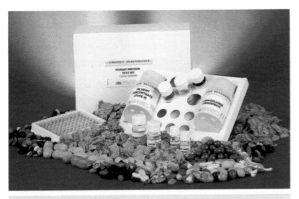

A peanut testing kit

Some companies use labels that state:

> *This product had been made in nut-free conditions using a nut-free recipe.*

Obesity

Obese people are seriously overweight. A government report in 1995 predicted that by 2005, 25% of British women and 18% of men will be obese. The causes of obesity are not clearly understood, but it is linked to a high-fat diet and lack of physical exercise. Many food products are clearly labelled to show their energy value and certain food products are designed for people who want to lose weight. The general guidelines for people who are on a 'slimming' or 'weight reducing' diet is to eat more starchy foods, cut down on fat and increase the amount of exercise they do.

Religion and food choices

Many religions have dietary guidelines that limit their food choices. Muslim food must be halal, which means that the animals are slaughtered according to Muslim law. Strict Jewish food must be kosher, which means that the food is prepared according to Jewish laws.

Questions

1 List three types of food intolerance or food allergy and in each case describe the food ingredients that people may need to avoid in their diet.

2 What advice would you give to people who want to lose weight?

3 Where can you find information to help people make food choices for special diets?

Key points

- People need information to help with food choices for special dietary needs.
- Products show information about gluten, nuts and other ingredients that need special care.

Vegetarian choices

About 3–4% of adults in the UK are vegetarian and the number of vegetarians seems to be increasing. Why do people become vegetarians?

- People do not like the thought that animals are killed for food.
- Certain religious groups eat a vegetarian diet.
- People are concerned about the environment and feel that meat production is expensive.
- People think a vegetarian diet is healthy.
- Many people enjoy the taste and the wide choice of vegetarian products.

Types of vegetarian

- Semi- or demi-vegetarians – don't eat red meat but will eat fish and poultry.
- Lacto-ovo vegetarians – don't eat meat, poultry or fish but will eat dairy products (milk, yogurt, butter, cheese) and eggs.
- Lacto vegetarians – don't eat meat, poultry, fish or eggs but will eat dairy products.
- Ovo vegetarians – don't eat meat, poultry, fish or dairy products, but will eat eggs.

- Vegans – don't eat meat, poultry, fish, dairy products or eggs.

Suitable for vegetarians?

How can you tell if a food product is suitable for a vegetarian? Many food producers have designed symbols to show that their food product is suitable for vegetarians. Some examples are shown opposite. The Vegetarian Society uses a V symbol to show that the ingredients are vegetarian and the product has been approved by them.

Food symbols for vegetarian products

Know your ingredients

When you are designing food for vegetarians, you need to check that the ingredients do not contain animal products.

Ingredients that need to be avoided or substituted to make food suitable for vegetarians

Ingredient	Changes for vegetarian choices
Gelatine – made from animal products	Look at the labels for jellies, yogurt, sweets and ice-cream and choose agar agar and vegetarian alternatives instead.
Fats for cakes and pastry	Use a vegetable fat instead of lard or butter, which are made from animal products.
Cheeses	Choose cheeses that state 'suitable for vegetarians'. The rennet used in other cheeses comes from animals. Avoid cheese altogether if cooking for vegans.
E numbers	E120 is made from cochineal (made from beetles), and E542 from edible bone phosphate so these should be avoided by vegetarians.
Vitamin D	Added vitamin D may come from lanolin in sheep's wool, so it is best to avoid products listing this as an added ingredient.
Worcester Sauce	Often made from anchovies so avoid as a flavouring.
Eggs	Some vegetarians prefer to eat free-range eggs. Processed foods usually contain eggs from battery farms.

The vegan diet

People who follow a vegan diet avoid meat, fish, eggs and dairy products but they still need a varied, balanced diet. Iron deficiency may be a problem for vegans as the most readily absorbed form of iron is found in red meat, offal, poultry and oily fish. The following foods are important iron sources for vegans: beans, peas and lentils, green leafy vegetables, dried fruit and fortified breakfast cereals. These foods should be eaten with a good source of vitamin C such as oranges and orange juice.

Vitamin B12 is needed to prevent a form of anaemia and is found naturally in foods from animal sources. Vegans may be advised to take vitamin B12 supplements or choose foods that have been fortified with B12 such as breakfast cereals. Calcium, needed for strong bones, is found in dairy products, which vegans do not eat. Vegans can choose soya milk and its products (which are fortified with calcium), bread and cereals, lentils and beans.

The vegan diet is very high in NSP (dietary fibre), which can prevent the absorption of calcium and other minerals. Vegans are advised not to eat too much unprocessed bran.

Meat replacements

Most new vegetarian products are based on meat replacements. There is a variety of meat replacement products which can be used when designing products for vegetarians, although varieties of beans, peas, lentils and tofu can supply sufficient protein in main dishes. Meat replacement products include TVP and the Quorn™ range.

- Tofu is made by curdling soya milk with calcium sulphate. The firm curd is called tofu. It needs to be eaten fresh. Tofu can be made into burgers, ready-meals and sausages. Silken tofu is like a thick cream. Tofu is a traditional food product popular in the Far East.

- TVP (textured vegetable protein) is made from soya bean flour with the fat removed. This flour is mixed to a dough with water and then forced through a small hole (extruded) under pressure at high temperature. TVP has a meat-like texture and can be made into burgers, burger mixes, sausages and ready-meals.

Quorn™ is a popular meat replacement

- The Quorn™ ingredient is mushroom in origin and is grown in a glucose-mix in a tall fermenting tower. It is mixed with vegetable-based flavourings, rolled into sheets and then set by steaming. Unlike many vegetarian products, it does not contain soya. Quorn™ can be sliced, diced or cut into chunks and made into meals such as curries, pies and stir-fries.

Questions

1 Explain why people choose to eat a vegetarian diet.

2 Create a day's menu for a vegan and explain how your choice provides a range of nutrients, especially iron, calcium and vitamin B12.

3 What is your view on the use of meat replacements in vegetarian dishes?

Key points

- Many new food products are designed and labelled to meet the needs of vegetarians.

- Vegans need to consider the nutritional balance of their diet.

- Meat replacements include TVP and Quorn™. Beans, peas and lentils provide nutrients suitable for a vegetarian diet.

Questions

[Food label section]

⊞	25 minutes

HEATING GUIDELINES

⊞ To Oven Cook

All cooking appliances vary in performance, these are guidelines only.
1. Preheat oven to 190°C, 375°F, Gas Mark 5.
2. Remove from carton and foil container.
3. Place on a baking tray on the middle oven shelf for 25 minutes.

From Frozen
Defrost thoroughly and follow guidelines from chilled.

¦O¦ To Serve Cold

This product is ready to eat. However, for best results, we recommend that you reheat it first and allow it to cool for 30 minutes before serving.

INGREDIENTS

MILK, EGG, WHEATFLOUR, VEGETARIAN CHEDDAR CHEESE, ONION, WHIPPING CREAM, VEGETARIAN FULL FAT SOFT CHEESE, HYDROGENATED AND NON-HYDROGENATED VEGETABLE OIL, VEGETABLE MARGARINE, MAIZE FLOUR, MODIFIED MAIZE STARCH, DIJON MUSTARD, POLYDEXTROSE, SALT, POTATO STARCH, WHITE PEPPER, VEGETABLE BOUILLON (WITH FLAVOURINGS).

*CONTAINS EGG, MILK, SOYA & WHEAT

❄ To Freeze

If freezing, freeze on day of purchase and consume within 1 month. Defrost thoroughly and use within 24 hours. Once thawed do not re-freeze.

NUTRITION INFORMATION
TYPICAL VALUES (cooked as per instructions)

	per ⅓ QUICHE	per 100g
ENERGY	1513 kJ.	1164 kJ.
	364 k cal	280 k cal
PROTEIN	11.3g	8.7g
CARBOHYDRATE	19.6g	15.1g
of which sugars	3.8g	2.9g
of which starch	15.9g	12.2g
FAT	26.7g	20.5g
of which saturates	12.5g	9.6g
of which mono-unsaturates	10.7g	8.2g
of which polyunsaturates	2.3g	1.8g
FIBRE	1.2g	0.9g
SODIUM	0.4g	0.3g

per ⅓ QUICHE	364 CAL	26.7 g FAT

GUIDELINE DAILY AMOUNTS

EACH DAY	WOMEN	MEN
CALORIES	2000	2500
FAT	70g	95g

RECOMMENDED BY NUTRITION PROFESSIONALS FOR AVERAGE ADULTS

⟨ 0044 7195 ⟩ P0688

If you are not entirely satisfied with this product please let us know on Sainsbury's Careline. Freephone 0800 636262

Your statutory rights are not affected.

PRODUCED IN THE UK FOR SAINSBURY'S SUPERMARKETS LTD. STAMFORD STREET LONDON SE1 9LL
INTERNET:
www.sainsburys.co.uk

A food label from Sainsbury's cheese and onion quiche

Use the label for cheese and onion quiche to answer questions 1–7.

1 This product states that it is suitable for vegetarians. List the ingredients that have been specially selected to meet the needs of vegetarians.

2 If the product did not have to be suitable for vegetarians, what ingredients could be used instead of the choices you have listed above?

3 The label provides information for people who may have food intolerances or allergies. List the ingredients in this product that people with food intolerances should avoid.

4 How could the product be made suitable for people with coeliac disease?

5 The label shows the Guideline Daily Amounts for calories and fat. Comment on the amount of calories and fat provided by one portion of this quiche (one-third of the quiche) in relation to the Guideline Daily Amounts.

6 Which ingredients provide the following nutrients:

    a protein

    b fat

    c carbohydrate

    d sodium

    e fibre (NSP or dietary fibre)?

7 Suggest how you could change the ingredients in this product if you wanted to lower the fat content and increase the amount of NSP (dietary fibre).

8 The chart below shows the fillings used for new chilled and savoury pies in the UK for 1997. Comment on why you think food companies are choosing to develop these types of filling.

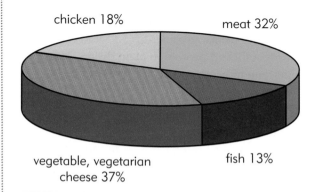

Fillings used for new chilled and savoury pies in the UK, 1997

Source: *New Products 1997*, Campden and Chorleywood Food Research Association

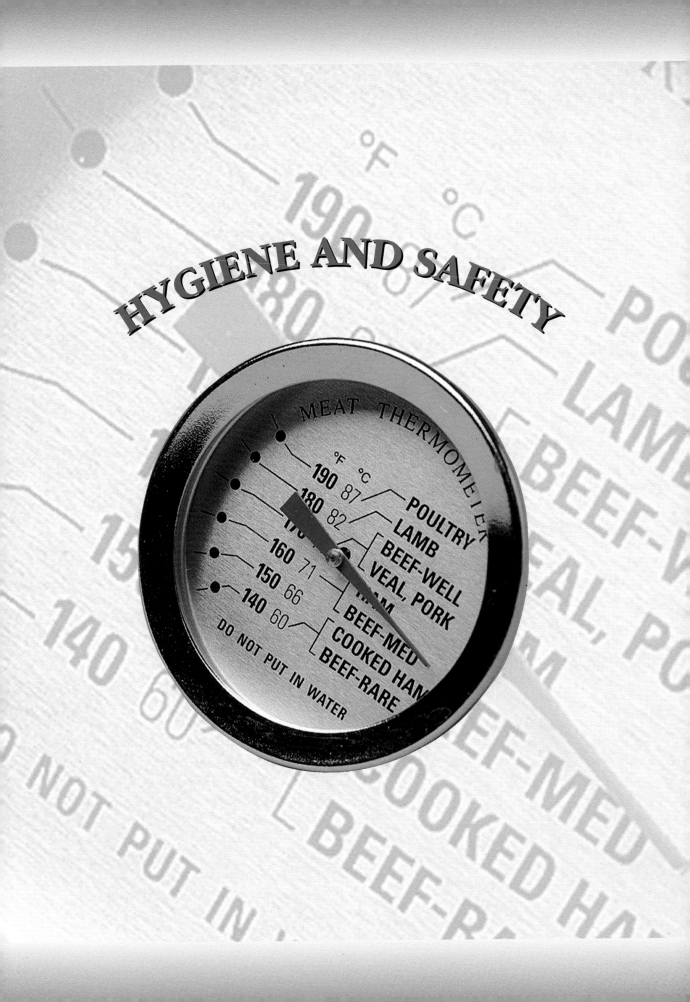

HYGIENE AND SAFETY

Hygiene and safety in the food industry

TRF pp.36, 37

5.1.6e, 5.1.9c, 5.2.5a, c

Safe and hygienic practices are essential for the preparation, cooking, transportation and storage of food ingredients and products. The food industry has legislation that protects the consumer which must be followed when making any food product to sell. Hygiene is essential throughout the food preparation chain when:

- choosing and buying food
- transporting the ingredients
- storing food
- preparing food
- cooking food
- keeping food warm or storing it.

These checklists are the same for small-scale food design or for larger food manufacturers.

Choosing and buying food

- Buy food from reputable suppliers who keep their food in safe conditions.
- Check that the food is within the datemark and check the 'use by' or 'best before' date.
- Choose food that looks fresh – vegetables should not be limp.
- Make sure perishable food is stored in cool conditions.

Transporting the ingredients

- Chilled, perishable food must be carried quickly from one area to another and it should be kept cool. The food industry uses insulated lorries to transport food.
- Frozen ingredients should be kept frozen. Special freezer lorries are used by industry.
- Other ingredients should be carried carefully so that they do not get damaged in transit.

Storing food

- Store food quickly after purchase, according to instructions. (Perishable and frozen food should be carried in cool bags.)
- It is good to practice to store frozen food at –18°C and chilled food at 5°C or below.
- Store raw and cooked foods separately.
- Food stored at **ambient temperature** should be covered and the room well ventilated.
- Store dry, packaged food, such as rice or flour, safely to avoid damp and pests.
- Cook-chill foods should be stored at low temperatures above freezing point (0° to 3°C) (see pages 70–1).

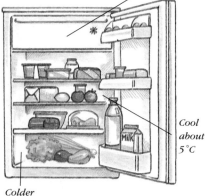

Freezing compartment –18°C and below

Cool about 5°C

Colder

Food should be correctly stored in a refrigerator

Preparing food

- Keep perishable food in the refrigerator for as long as possible during food preparation.
- Defrost frozen food before preparation unless label says otherwise.
- Clean all surfaces before and after working with food.
- Wash all fruit and vegetables before use.
- Take special care when preparing raw meat and poultry – use separate equipment and wipe down the area after preparation is finished. Wash your hands to avoid **cross-contamination**.

- Colour coded chopping boards are used in industry to help avoid cross-contamination from one food product to another. Raw meat must be prepared separately from cooked meat, so it is good practice to use a red board for raw meat and a yellow board for cooked meat.

- In industry, vegetables are washed with special cleansing agents before they are used in food products. For example, Veggi Wash produces a clean and safe product.

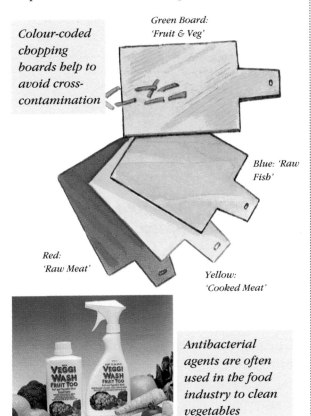

Colour-coded chopping boards help to avoid cross-contamination

Green Board: 'Fruit & Veg'

Blue: 'Raw Fish'

Red: 'Raw Meat'

Yellow: 'Cooked Meat'

Antibacterial agents are often used in the food industry to clean vegetables

Cooking food and keeping food warm

- Make sure food is thoroughly cooked.
- Food should be cooked to 70°C for at least 2 minutes.
- Hot food should be kept at or above 63°C.

Storing cooked food

- Cool food quickly if you do not want to eat it immediately.

Temperature control

Check that refrigerators and freezers are working at the right temperature by using a refrigerator thermometer or a temperature probe. The temperature probe can be used to test the temperature of cooked dishes as well as foods stored in the refrigerator.

The temperature of food can easily be tested using one of these probes

Questions

1 Explain why it is useful to use different coloured cutting boards for food preparation. List the colours of the cutting boards and state which type of food should be prepared on each type of board.

2 If you were buying the following ingredients for cooking and eating, list the stages in the food chain that need special care to make the product safe to eat.

   a Buying frozen ice-cream and getting it from the shop to the table for eating.

   b Buying eggs to make into omelettes.

   c Buying minced beef to make into beefburgers.

   d Buying frozen chicken nuggets to make into a meal.

Key points

- Good hygiene is essential throughout the food preparation chain.
- Rules and regulations support the preparation of food so that it is safe to eat.

Safety in the food chain

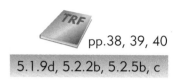
Food hygiene

All food workers must be properly dressed and prepared before they start working with food ingredients. The food industry has strict hygiene rules for people to follow.

Getting ready for food work

- Hair should be tied back and covered with a hat or net.
- Wear clean, protective clothing such as an overall, apron and special footwear.
- Remove all jewellery including earrings and rings.
- Cover any cuts with waterproof dressings. The food industry uses blue dressings so that they can be easily seen if they fall into food.

Special clothing is worn in the high- and low-risk areas at Noon Products plc. Blue is chosen for hairnets, hats and disposable gloves because they can be seen if they accidentally fall into food. Special boots are worn in each area and the overalls show which area the person is working in

Preparing to work

- Wash your hands with water and anti-bacterial soap before working with food.
- Dry your hands using a hot-air dryer.
- Always wash your hands if you have been to the toilet or left the food preparation area.
- Do not touch your face, hair or nose during food preparation.
- Do not cough or sneeze over food or lick your fingers or smoke in a food preparation area.
- If you are feeling sick do not work with food until you are well.

Case study of hygiene testing in a cannelloni factory

The cannelloni in this case study is a chilled ready-meal made from fresh egg pasta with beef and tomato filling and a creamy sauce topped with Parmesan cheese.

Getting ready for work in the food industry

The food industry has strict rules on clothing and hygiene procedures. Employees must wear a hairnet, cap, overalls, wellington boots but no watches or dangling jewellery. Before they enter the food area they must wash their hands and use an alcohol rub, then walk through a sanitized bath to clean their boots. People may wash their hands between 20–30 times each shift. In the **low-risk area,** the uniform is green wellingtons and in the **high-risk area** the uniform is white wellingtons and often a red stripe on overalls.

Before employment, employees must have a faeces test to make sure they are safe to work in the food industry and this test must be repeated if they are ill. This test will identify if the person has been contaminated with food poisoning bacteria.

Testing for food hygiene

The factory has a microbiological laboratory where the raw materials are tested for safety. Swabs are taken from the production line, which is stopped and cleaned once an hour with sanitizing fluid. Swabs are taken from employees' hands in unannounced checks. The cannelloni is tested three times a day as some bacteria are found in any food and the results must meet specified levels. Tests are conducted every week for *Salmonella*, *Listeria* and other pathogens.

Industrial practice

In industry, **systems** are set up to control and monitor the storage and **shelf life** of food products used in food production. These systems ensure that food is not out of date and that the storage areas are operating effectively. Any food that is out of date must be thrown away.

McDonald's stock control

At McDonald's, stock control is very important to maintain high standards of food safety.

Storage temperature and recommended shelf life for some McDonald's products

Product	Storage temperature	Recommended shelf life
Regular buns	ambient	4 days
Cheese slices	2–4°C	6 weeks
Bulk ketchup	ambient	4 months
Ketchup portions	ambient	2 months
Lettuce	2–4°C	5 days
Meat patties	–18 to –23°C	6 weeks
Mustard	ambient	2 months
Onions (fresh)	2–4°C	5 days
Onions (dehydrated)	ambient	6 months
Pickles	ambient	2 months
Big Mac sauce	2–4°C	60 days
Tomatoes (fresh)	ambient	approx 6 days

Source: *Food 2000*, McDonald's

Some definitions	
Swabs	samples taken from areas using a small scraper to remove a layer for analysis
Pathogens	dangerours bacteria
Sanitizing fluid	cleaning liquid that can remove bacteria

Questions

1 Give three reasons why is it important for food workers to prepare themselves carefully before working with food.

2 Look at the case study for the cannelloni factory. Explain how the factory carries out tests for the safety of their food products.

3 What procedures must be carried out before workers enter the food preparation area? Explain why these procedures are important.

Look at the McDonald's table to answer the following questions.

4 List the foods that need to be stored at:

   a ambient temperature

   b chilled temperature (2–4°C)

   c frozen temperature.

   Explain why each of these foods is stored at that temperature.

5 Which foods have:

   a the longest recommended shelf life?

   b the shortest recommended shelf life?

   Explain why these foods have a long or short shelf life.

Key points

● From purchase to preparation, foods must be stored safely and correctly.

● Food factories have strict rules for hygiene and food preparation.

Food and the law

TRF pp.41–42

5.1.9c, 5.2.2b, 5.2.5b, d, e

There are several laws that protect consumers and workers in the food industry. These are the important Acts that concern the food industry:

- Consumer Protection Act 1987
- Sale of Goods Act 1979
- Trade Descriptions Act 1968
- Weights and Measures Act 1985
- Food Safety (General Food Hygiene) Regulations 1995
- Food Safety (Temperature Control) Regulations 1995
- Food Safety Act 1990
- Food Labelling Regulations 1996, amended 1998 and 1999
- Health and Safety at Work Act 1974
- Management of Health and Safety at Work Regulations 1999
- Control of Substances Hazardous to Health Regulations 1999 (COSSH)
- Reporting of Injuries, Diseases and Dangerous Occurrences Regulations (RIDDOR '95)
- Provision and Use of Work Equipment Regulations 1998
- Electricity at Work Regulations 1989
- First Aid at Work Regulations 1981
- Food Premises (Registration) Regulations 1991.

Protecting the consumer

These are the Acts that protect the consumer when buying products:

- the Consumer Protection Act 1987 protects the consumer from being given misleading details on the price of products and services
- the Sale of Goods Act 1979, 1994 and the Sale and Supply of Goods Act 1994 state that products must be of satisfactory quality, fit for their purpose and as described

- the Trade Descriptions Act 1968 makes it an offence to make false or misleading statements about products or mislead consumers about services, accommodation or facilities
- the Weights and Measures Act 1985 makes it an offence to sell underweight products or to mark products with the wrong amount.

Trading standards officers

These people work for the local authority and help to protect the consumer from unfair trading. They make sure that products are properly labelled and show the correct weight and product information. They visit factories and shops to inspect measuring equipment, and can test food samples at any stage of the production and selling process.

Environmental health officers

These people also work for the local authority and are responsible for public health issues such as the hygiene of food businesses and food safety. Environmental health officers investigate cases of microbial contamination of foods, and foods that are unfit for human consumption. This meets the requirements of the Food Safety Act 1990.

An environmental health officer at work

Protecting our food

These are some of the important Acts that help to make our food safe to eat.

The Food Safety (General Food Hygiene) Regulations 1995

These regulations lay down standards for premises, equipment and personal hygiene to ensure the safety and wholesomeness of food. The regulations cover the preparation, processing, manufacturing, packaging, storing, transportation, distribution, handling and selling of food products.

Areas included in the regulations are:

- **hazard** analysis and risk assessment
- food hygiene training.

Anyone handling food must be able to prove they have shown **due diligence** in food preparation and have set up systems to help avoid food contamination.

The Food Safety (Temperature Control) Regulations 1995

The regulations require high risk, perishable foods to be kept at or below 8°C, and cooked or reheated food that needs to be hot must be kept at a temperature at or above 63°C.

The Food Safety Act 1990

This is designed to help reduce the number of cases of food-borne illness such as food poisoning and contamination. It is an offence to sell any food that is harmful to health, contaminated, falsely labelled or falsely advertised. Failure to meet these requirements can result in unlimited fines and/or imprisonment.

The Food Labelling Regulations 1999

These describe the information that must be on a food label. See page 101 for more information.

Protecting people who work in the food industry

There are several acts and regulations that protect people when they are at work.

- COSSH Regulations provide a system to help control hazardous substances in all types of business, including food businesses, and so protect the workforce from working in a harmful environment. In the food industry, hazardous substances can include the use of pesticides and cleaning agents in a food factory.

- The Health and Safety at Work Act makes employers responsible for the health and safety of their workforce. The Health and Safety Executive has inspectors who visit businesses to check that the Act is being followed. Employers must carry out a risk assessment of the workplace to find out what the risks are and the likely way to tackle them.

- RIDDOR '95 requires the reporting of work-related accidents, diseases and dangerous occurrences. Reporting accidents and ill health at work is a legal requirement and it helps to identify how risks arise and provides evidence for investigations into serious accidents.

Questions

1. Describe the work of the following people:
   a. trading standards officers
   b. environmental health officers.
2. Why do you think this work is important?
3. Write briefly about the Food Safety (General Food Hygiene) Regulations 1995.
4. What is meant by the term 'due diligence'?
5. Which regulations and laws help the consumer to buy safe food?

Key points

- Many laws protect consumers and help to provide safe food.
- Laws protect workers in the food industry.

Food poisoning

TRF p.43

5.2.1f, i, 5.2.5c

Bacteria

Bacteria are the most common cause of food poisoning. Food poisoning bacteria cause vomiting, diarrhoea, stomach cramps, fever and any combination of these symptoms. Some food poisoning bacteria even cause death.

In the right conditions, bacteria can multiply by splitting in two every 10–20 minutes. In just 45 minutes, one bacterium will have multiplied to one million bacteria. To grow and multiply bacteria need four things:

- warmth
- food
- moisture
- time.

Warmth

Bacteria thrive at temperatures around 37°C – our body temperature. Bacteria will grow at any temperature between 5°C and 63°C. This temperature range is known as the **danger zone**. Food should be kept above or below the danger zone to limit the time bacteria can multiply.

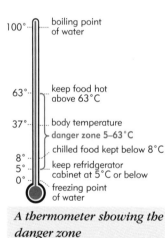

100° — boiling point of water
63° — keep food hot above 63°C
37° — body temperature
danger zone 5–63°C
chilled food kept below 8°C
8°
5° — keep refridgerator cabinet at 5°C or below
0° — freezing point of water

A thermometer showing the danger zone

Temperatures above 70°C will destroy most bacteria, so food should be cooked until it is piping hot – hotter than 70°C for 2 minutes.

Moisture

Bacteria need moisture (liquid) to grow, which is one reason why dried foods have a long shelf life. If foods have high levels of sugar (for example, jams), high levels of acid (for example, pickles) or salt (for example, salami) then the water in the foods is not available for the bacteria to grow.

Food

Bacteria prefer foods that are high in protein and moist. These **high-risk foods** include meat, poultry, eggs and fish. High-risk foods also include mayonnaise, cooked rice and dairy products.

Time

Bacteria can multiply quickly in a very short time in the right conditions, so food must not be left in warm conditions for very long.

Dangers

Food-poisoning bacteria can pass from one area to another by cross-contamination. Examples of cross-contamination include:

- raw food touching cooked food
- blood or juices from raw meat dripping on to cooked food
- bacteria being transferred from one food to another on hands, tools and equipment.

The most common danger points in food handling are:

- not cooking food thoroughly – for example, not cooking raw chicken sufficiently on a barbecue
- preparing food long before it is needed and keeping it in warm conditions
- cross-contamination from a raw food to a cooked food
- not thawing food properly such as frozen chicken
- not storing chilled food in a refrigerator.

The food poisoning chain

Food poisoning bacteria contaminate food and the bacteria multiply over a period of time to a dangerous level. People eat this food and become ill with food poisoning.

Types of bacteria

There are many types of food-poisoning bacteria, each one with its own symptoms and food sources. Most bacteria are killed by thorough heating, but some, such as *Clostridium botulinum*, produce spores which survive high cooking temperatures.

Food poisoning bacteria	Likely sources
Salmonella	Many types of raw meat, poultry and eggs
Campylobacter	Raw poultry and other meats
Listeria	Soft cheeses and patés
Escherichia coli	Raw meat
Clostridium perfringens	Raw meat, vegetables, herbs and spices
Clostridium botulinum	Spores form toxin
Staphylococcus aureus	Food handlers
Bacillus cereus	Pre-cooked rice dishes and other grains

Cases of food poisoning

The Public Health Laboratory Service's Communicable Disease Surveillance Centre provides statistics on the number of reported cases of food poisoning each year. You can look up this information on the Internet at http:\\www.phls.co.uk.

All doctors must notify the local authority of cases, or suspected cases, of food poisoning. The table shows the change in numbers of reported cases in recent years.

Reported cases of food poisoning in England and Wales, 1991–99

Year	Total reported cases
1991	52,543
1992	63,347
1993	68,587
1994	81,833
1995	82,041
1996	83,233
1997	93,901
1998	93,932
1999	86,316

The number of cases has risen since 1991 for several reasons:

● doctors are reporting more cases as they know about the system

● food poisoning is on the increase.

The food industry is concerned about outbreaks of food poisoning. If the problem can be traced back to the food or catering company, the company may be fined and business will suffer.

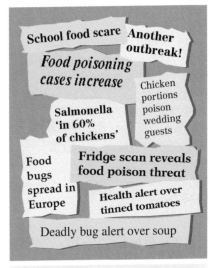

Food poisoning frequently hits the headlines

Questions

1 Look at the chart showing the reported cases of food poisoning. Comment on the findings.

2 Draw a graph to show the reported cases of food poisoning since 1991. You can check the Internet for the most recent figures.

3 What are the most common danger points in food handling?

Key points

● Bacteria need warmth, moisture, food and time to grow and multiply.

● Cases of food poisoning are increasing.

Temperature control

Temperature control is the most effective way to control bacteria.

Keep food cool

If food is kept cool in a refrigerator, the bacteria are not killed, but their growth is slowed down. Refrigerators should operate at 5°C or below. This can be checked using a refrigerator thermometer. In the food and catering industry the temperature of refrigerated storerooms is constantly checked to avoid dangerous temperature rises.

A refrigerator thermometer

Frozen food

Domestic freezers operate at –18°C or below. Industrial freezers used by canteens or supermarkets should operate at –29°C. Freezers stop bacteria growing but do not kill them, so once the food is defrosted, the bacteria can multiply in warm conditions.

Food Hygiene Regulations require that most short life food is stored at 8°C or colder when it is being processed, during distribution and in display in shops.

Cook food to a high enough temperature

Bacteria are destroyed at high temperatures, so if food is thoroughly heated to at least 70°C at its centre for 2 minutes, harmful micro-organisms, including bacteria will be destroyed. Food can be tested using a temperature probe to see if a high enough temperature has been reached.

Cool food quickly

If food is to be reheated (e.g. **cook-chill** meals) it must be cooled as quickly as possible. In industry, food is blast-chilled after it has been cooked, to chill it really quickly.

Reheating food

Reheated food, such as microwave meals, must be cooked to 70°C for 2 minutes. If you are designing a food product that will be reheated in the microwave, you must test to find out how long it should be cooked to reach this temperature. Put this information on the food label as part of the serving instructions.

The Food Safety (Temperature Control) Regulations require perishable foods to be kept at or below 8°C and cooked or reheated food that needs to be hot must be kept at a temperature at or above 63°C.

Using a food probe

Hand-held temperature probes are useful for testing the temperature of food

Food probes are used to measure food temperature. There are many types of probe and some can be linked to a computer to monitor temperature changes. Insert the probe to a depth of 2 cm into the food. Wait for the temperature display to settle, then record the reading. Each time the probe is used, wipe it with a bacterial food wipe. This will reduce the risk of cross-contamination of bacteria from one food to another.

In the food industry, sensors linked to computers monitor temperature changes in freezers, refrigerators, chill cabinets, ovens, cooling racks and storage facilities.

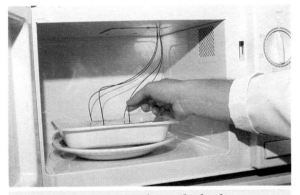

Optic fibres are inserted into the food

Testing microwave cooking instructions

Extensive testing must be carried out by the food industry to make sure that the times given for reheating products in the microwave are sufficient to heat the foods to a safe high temperature. In a test kitchen, special optic fibres are inserted into the food inside the microwave oven. The food is heated and the temperature changes are monitored through the optic fibres, which are linked to a computer system. When the correct temperature is reached, the computer prints out a record of the test, which is kept in case the measurements are challenged.

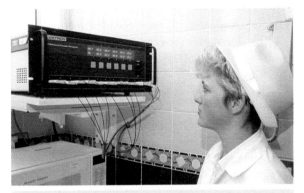

The temperatures during cooking are recorded on a computer system

From factory to supermarket

The temperature of chilled products must be carefully controlled at all stages from the factory to the supermarket. The products are transported in chilled lorries to the distribution centre by lorry to the store. Temperature records are kept at every stage in the delivery process. The products are taken from the store to the chiller cabinets or freezer areas. No products must be left out of chill for more than 20 minutes. The chiller cabinets contain thermometers which monitor the temperature inside the cabinet.

Questions

1 List the different storage areas for chilled food. What temperature should the following operate at:

  a the refrigerator

  b the freezer?

2 To destroy bacteria, what temperature should food be heated to?

3 How is temperature monitored in the food industry?

4 Explain why temperature control is important.

Key points

● Temperature control is an effective way to control bacteria.

● The food industry monitors temperature during production and distribution.

Questions

Food poisoning hits 9.5m a year, 100 times the official estimate

Food poisoning is claiming 9.5 million victims a year, a secret government report reveals. Officially, the number of registered cases of food poisoning is 100,000 a year but not everyone reports the illness. The report suggests the total should be multiplied by 100. The cost to the economy is put at £743 million a year in lost working hours and medical treatment.

The main cause of food poisoning, such as Salmonella and E. coli have generally been attributed to disease among farm animals and failures in food handling. A high proportion of chickens are contaminated with Salmonella and Campylobacter, which can survive if the birds are not cooked properly. Eggs can also be contaminated with Salmonella, which may be transmitted to humans.

Much of the blame has been put on methods of preparation in the home. But leaks from the report suggest that people are no more careless than they have ever been.

Adapted from: *Daily Mail*, 19 November 1998

Use the article to answer questions 1–4.

1 Why does the article suggest that the number of food poisoning cases is more than the registered figures?

2 What are the main causes of food poisoning?

3 From what you have read previously, list ways that food hygiene in the home can be improved.

4 The report says that 'people are no more careless than they have ever been'. Explain in your own words why the cases of food poisoning might be increasing.

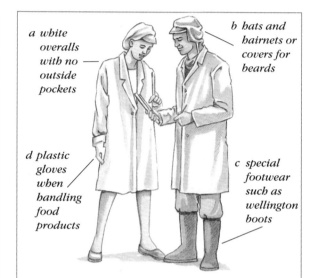

a white overalls with no outside pockets

b hats and hairnets or covers for beards

d plastic gloves when handling food products

c special footwear such as wellington boots

5 Food workers need to wear special protective clothes for food work. Explain why each of the items of clothing labelled **a–d** on the picture are worn.

6 Make a list of dos and don'ts for people working in a food preparation area. For example, 'Do not smoke'.

Packing airline meals at an airport

7 The picture shows food being packed for airline meals. Make a list of all the hygiene and safety procedures that you can find in this picture.

FOOD INGREDIENTS

Properties and functions

TRF pp.45–46, 47–48

5.2.1a, d, e, f, 5.2.3b

We need to eat a variety of foods to provide the range of nutrients we need for a balanced diet. When you design food products the ingredients are chosen for their special function in the product **formulation** or recipe. When you choose ingredients for a product you are thinking about their function as well as their nutritional value. The composition of different types of food gives it characteristics and working properties (functions) to thicken, set, aerate and coagulate when part of a recipe.

Functions of ingredients

These are some **key words** and terms to describe the functions of ingredients in a product:

> flavour, colour, bulk, taste, sweetness, preservative properties, lightens mixtures, moistens, forms a structure, sets food, thickens sauces, adds texture, shortens baked food.

Aerate

Wholemeal bread

Cakes

Baking powder is used to make cakes rise

Yeast makes bread rise

Glaze

Ham

Pie

Egg is used to glaze pastry

Honey glazes the top of roast ham

Bind

Pastry

Fish Cakes

Egg binds the ingredients

Water binds together flour and fat for pastry

Set

Egg flan

Cold soufflé

Gelatine helps form the structure

Egg sets in a flan

Bulk

Crumble

Meat loaf

Flour is used in the topping

Bread is used to bulk out the recipe

Thicken

Soup

Sauce

Cornflour is used to thicken sauces

Flour thickens soups

Adapted from original material developed by the British Nutritional Foundation

Properties or functions	Examples
Adding	Food should be attractive and colourful. You can improve the look of a dish, for example by adding a garnish of parsley to a white sauce, or a cherry on top of a dessert.
Adding flavour to foods	Salt, pepper, herbs and spices all help to improve the flavour of savoury dishes. Strong flavoured foods such as bacon and tomatoes add flavour to sauces. For sweet foods you can add chocolate, nuts and dried fruits. You may want to add a delicate flavour such as vanilla to an ice-cream.
Adding textures	Sometimes you may want to add another food for texture such as adding a crunchy salad to a smooth pasta dish. Foods such as peas provide colour and texture to a rice dish, and fresh fruit pieces improve the texture of a yogurt or milky dessert.
Aerating	Many foods need to be made lighter by adding a gas such as air, carbon dioxide or steam. This can be done by whisking certain ingredients such as eggs to introduce air, adding raising agents such as yeast to introduce carbon dioxide gas or using liquid such as milk in batter to introduce steam when the product is cooked.
Binding	Some ingredients need binding together such as those for beefburgers, vegetable burgers and pastry. You can use water and eggs to bind things together and other ingredients such as flour will help the ingredients to stick together.
Bulking	Some foods are used for bulk – they make up the main part of the recipe. Flour is a good bulking agent used in bread and pastry. Oats are used as the bulking agent in muesli, and rice is the main food in risotto.
Emulsifying	Ingredients such as eggs help other liquids hold together such as when making mayonnaise from oil and vinegar.
Preserving	Ingredients can help other foods to keep longer. Sugar is needed for jam making to preserve the fruit, vinegar for pickles to preserve the vegetables and salt for salting fish to increase the keeping time.
Setting food	Foods such as jellies and cold sauces are set by using a variety of ingredients. Gelatine is used to set jelly. Cold sauces such as blancmange are set with cornflour and other sauces may use other starch products such as flour.
Shortening	Ingredients such as fats and oils help to shorten a flour mixture such as pastry and make it crisp or crumbly in texture.
Sweetening	Many foods can be used to sweeten dishes, but the main ingredient used is sugar. Dried fruits that add sweetness include raisins, sultanas and apricots. Honey and preserves such as jam can be used to sweeten desserts, and fresh fruits can be added to foods such as muesli for sweetness.
Thickening	Sauces, soups and stews may need thickening, so you can use a variety of flours or starchy vegetables or bread to thicken the sauce or soup.

Question

1 Look at the functions illustrated above (aerate, thicken, set, bind, bulk and glaze).

a List as many other ingredients as you can that perform one or more of these functions.

b For each ingredient you have listed, name a food product or recipe that uses the ingredient.

Key points

- Food ingredients have a function within the recipe.
- Food ingredients may perform several functions in one recipe.

Nutrition and cooking

Heating and nutrition changes

This chart shows the effects of heating on nutrients and the changes in the nutritional value. Similar changes take place during food processing.

	Effects of heating	How is this used in the cooking process?	Nutritional changes
Starch	1 With dry heat starch turns to dextrin. 2 With liquid, starch granules soften and swell and absorb water and thicken liquids (gelatinization).	1 Toasting bread to make it crispy, golden breadcrumbs, the crust of bread. 2 Thickening soups, sauces and custards.	The carbohydrate value is not lost unless the food is burnt.
Sugar	When heated sugar dissolves, it changes from white to golden, caramelizes and eventually burns.	Used to make syrups and caramel for caramel custard.	The carbohydrate value is not lost unless the food is burnt.
Fats – solid	Melt to a liquid, bubble and can decompose at high temperatures when fats give off smoke and burn. Fats have different melting and decomposition temperatures. Low fat spreads contain a lot of water and are not usually used in cooking.	Solid fats are used for frying. Butter is used to fry onions – it melts and bubbles but must not be heated to a high temperature as it burns and blackens.	Fat is not changed in value during cooking unless the fat is burnt.
Protein	Protein denatures (changes) on heating, then coagulates and sets.	Eggs go through various changes as they are fried, boiled or poached, and eventually become solid. Meat hardens and browns.	The protein value is not lost in cooking unless the food is burnt.
Vitamins – fat soluble (A and D)	Fat-soluble vitamins are not affected by the cooking process. They are not soluble in water so are not lost when food is cooked in water or soaked.		Fat-soluble vitamins are not lost during cooking.
Vitamins – water soluble (B and C)	Because these vitamins are water soluble they dissolve in cooking water. High temperature cooking during frying and baking destroys these vitamins.	Vitamin C is easily lost during preparation and cooking of vegetables. Avoid long cooking and keeping vegetables warm.	Water-soluble vitamins can be lost during cooking. Vitamin C is lost if fruit and vegetables are stored for too long.
NSP (dietary fibre)	NSP (dietary fibre) softens when it is heated with liquid.	Boiled cabbage becomes soft on cooking in water.	NSP (dietary fibre) remains indigestible after cooking.
Minerals	Heating has little effect on the minerals in food.		There is little mineral loss during preparation and cooking.

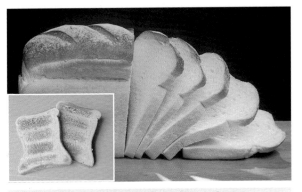

Heat turns the starch in bread into dextrin, making the crust of a loaf crispy and turning a slice of bread golden brown when toasted

Sugar turns brown when it is heated to a high temperature. The sugar topping on this crème brûlée has been browned under the grill or with a blow torch

Heating an egg coagulates the protein, which changes the consistency and colour of the egg

Experiment to test the coagulation temperature of an egg

When eggs are heated the protein in the white and the yolk coagulates, and the white and the yolk thicken. The appearance and texture of the egg changes.

These are the facts:

- thin egg white around the outside of the egg coagulates at about 63°C

- the remaining egg white begins to thicken and whiten at 66°C

- the egg yolk begins to thicken at 65°C and becomes solid at about 70°C.

You need:

- water
- an egg
- a frying pan
- a food probe.

Method

1. Heat a little water in a frying pan. Crack the egg into the water.

2. Continue heating the pan and measure the temperature of the different parts of the egg as the protein coagulates.

3. Compare your results with the facts listed.

4. Heat the egg for longer and notice the changes in the texture.

yolk — thick white — thin white

The different parts of an egg yolk coagulate at different temperatures

Questions

1. Describe the changes that take place when the following nutrients are heated:

   a starch

   b sugar

   c solid fat

   d protein.

2. What changes occur when different vitamins and minerals are heated?

Key point

- Different nutrients change in a variety of ways during cooking and processing.

Cereals

The most common cereals are wheat, barley, maize, rye and oats. Different types of food made from cereals include bread, breakfast cereals, pasta and noodles. The main nutrients in cereals are carbohydrate in the form of starch, some protein, NSP (dietary fibre) and some calcium, iron and B vitamins.

Products made from cereals and how they are processed

Type of cereal	Products made with this cereal	Processed forms of cereal sold
Wheat	bread, pasta, pastry, biscuits, pies, cakes	flour, wheat flakes, semolina
Oats	biscuits, porridge, oatcakes, bread, muesli	oat flakes or rolled oats, oatmeal, oatbran, flour
Maize	bread, popcorn, sweetcorn vegetable, cornflour, polenta	cornflour, polenta, cornmeal, hominy, popcorn
Rye	rye bread, rye crispbread, muesli	flour, rye flakes, bran
Rice	ready-meals such as rice with curry, Chinese dishes with rice, noodles, rice cakes, puddings	whole grains, flour, ground rice
Barley	soft drinks, beer, scones	barley flakes, whole grain barley, pearl barley, flour

Other cereals include millet, buckwheat and sorghum. For healthy eating we are encouraged to eat wholemeal, wholegrain, brown or high-NSP (dietary fibre) versions of cereals where possible.

Wheat

Wheat is the most important cereal used in the UK. The wheat grain is made up of three important parts, which are used for different flours:

- bran
  12% of the wheat – the outside coat of the wheat – a good source of NSP (dietary fibre)
- wheatgerm
  3% of the wheat – contains nutritious vitamins and oils
- endosperm
  85% of the wheat – the white part, containing starch and protein.

The grain of wheat is milled and each stage needs to be checked for quality

Types of wheat flour	Uses
White flour (75% of wheat grain) Plain Strong white flour made from hard wheat Self-raising flour	used for thickening sauces and pastry used for breadmaking used to help cakes and biscuits rise
Wholewheat or wholemeal flour (100% flour from the whole grain)	more nutritious than white flour and used for breads and pastries
Stoneground flour (100% flour and whole grain)	good flavour and used for breads and pastries
Malted wheat flour	a brown flour with a nutty flavour from added malted wheat grains

Pasta

Pasta is made by mixing together flour and water to form a paste. Italian pasta is made from durum wheat semolina, which is a hard variety of wheat. It is higher in protein than other varieties, and makes a pasta that is golden in colour and retains its shape and texture during cooking.

Nutrition

Pasta is a good source of carbohydrate and contains some protein, NSP (dietary fibre), B vitamins, potassium and iron. Wholewheat pasta made from the whole wheat grain provides more NSP (dietary fibre) than refined, white pasta. This pale brown pasta takes longer to cook than the refined produce because of its NSP (dietary fibre) content.

Coloured pasta

Pasta can be coloured with a variety of ingredients. Green lasagne and tagliatelle are coloured with spinach juice or powder. Tomato purée makes a pale pink pasta, saffron or turmeric makes yellow pasta and chocolate powder a dark brown pasta. Dried pasta will keep for many months whereas fresh pasta needs to be eaten within a few days.

Rice

Different kinds of rice are used to make different products. Long grain rice is used for savoury dishes, especially in Indian and Chinese cooking. Short grain rice is used for puddings.

Cereals as part of meals

Around the world people use a range of cereals as starchy accompaniments with main meals. Couscous with vegetable stew, rice with curry, pasta with sauce, noodles with stir-fried vegetables, polenta with stew.

Changing the recipe formulation

You can change the variety of cereals in a recipe to improve the product. For example, breads can be made from different types of flour.

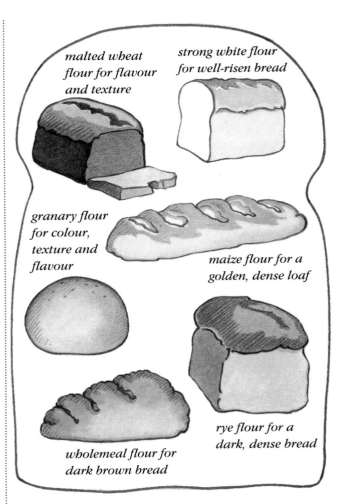

malted wheat flour for flavour and texture

strong white flour for well-risen bread

granary flour for colour, texture and flavour

maize flour for a golden, dense loaf

wholemeal flour for dark brown bread

rye flour for a dark, dense bread

Questions

1 Name three different types of wheat flour and explain how each is used in cooking.

2 Choose a flour for making bread and give reasons for your choice. Suggest an alternative choice with reasons.

3 Suggest the types of pasta (the shapes and colours) that you would use with a tomato sauce. Give reasons for your choice.

4 Make a list of cereals that are served as accompaniments with meals.

Key points

- Cereals are important foods in our diet.
- Cereals are used in a wide variety of products.

Cereals in cooking

Starchy foods made from wheat and other cereals have an important function in many recipes. These cereals are often pounded into flour.

Types of flour

Different cereals produce different types of flour:

- wheat flour from wheat
- cornflour made from maize
- potato flour from potatoes
- rice flour from rice
- arrowroot made from a tropical root.

Most types of flour are mainly made up of the carbohydrate starch. This changes during cooking and affects the cooking properties.

What happens when starch is heated in a liquid?

Starch needs to be cooked because raw starch tastes floury and is not easily digested. When starch and water are heated, the water passes through the walls of the starch granules and the granules become swollen and may burst. This process is called gelatinization – a process in which starch, on heating, absorbs water and thickens liquids. This process is used to thicken sauces and soups.

If gelatinization does not take place properly you can end up with:

- a lumpy sauce
- a raw, uncooked starch taste
- a sauce with the wrong consistency.

How gelatinization is used to thicken liquids

- Wheat flour is used with butter or margarine and milk to make a thick white sauce. Wheat flour gives a cloudy, creamy sauce and is used for white sauces and soups.
- Arrowroot is blended with water or fruit juice then heated until it thickens and used to glaze fruit on flans. Arrowroot gives a clear transparent sauce.
- Cornflour gives a less clear, more opaque gel and is used for sweet and savoury sauces.

Heat starch granules in water *Starch granules become swollen*

Starch granules burst *The liquid thickens and gelatinizes*

Starch gelatinizes when heated in a liquid, producing a thickened liquid

If the thickened liquid is left to cool, it will set and form a gel. For example, custard powder (made from coloured cornflour) thickens when heated with milk. When it cools, it sets and is used for the top of trifles and sweet desserts. Blancmange is made from flavoured, coloured cornflour, which is blended and then heated with milk and sugar and sometimes set in a mould.

Acid foods such as tomatoes and lemon juice break down the starch granules slightly. This lowers the thickening power of the starch in a sauce.

Gluten

Many cereals contain gluten, the protein that forms the structure of bread, cakes and pasta. People with coeliac disease need to avoid foods containing gluten.

Gluten in flour

When water is added to flour, the proteins in the flour form into another protein, called gluten. The amount of gluten varies with the type of flour. Strong flours used for breadmaking contain the most gluten. When flour mixtures are heated, the air, steam or carbon dioxide push up the mixture and the gluten strands set, providing the structure of the baked goods.

When designing recipes for biscuits and cakes, you need to find out if the flour that you are using provides any gluten. Here is a simple test.

Compare the amount of gluten in different flours

You need:

- a range of flours (e.g. wheat, potato, maize, sorghum, rye, barley)
- scales
- water
- mixing bowls
- J cloths
- baking tray.

Method

1 Mix 100 g of each flour with enough water to form a dough and knead until smooth.

2 Wrap each ball of dough in a J cloth. Hold it under the tap and run water over the dough.

3 The starchy liquid runs out into the water. Wash until no more starch runs out.

4 If there is gluten in the flour, it will be left inside the J cloth. Bake the gluten balls in a hot oven at 220°C (gas mark 7) until each ball is puffed up and golden brown. Compare the size of the cooked gluten balls. Comment on your results.

Which type of flour produced the biggest gluten ball when baked?

Questions

1 Explain what happens to starch when it is heated in liquid.

2 How can you measure the thickness of a sauce?

3 Why is it useful to know if a cereal contains gluten?

4 How can gluten be detected in products?

Key points

- Starch gelatinizes on heating. This is used to thicken liquids.
- Some cereals contain gluten which forms the structure of products such as bread.

Fruit and vegetables

Do you eat five portions a day?

For a healthy diet, we are advised to eat five portions of fruit and vegetables a day. These portions can be fresh, frozen, dried, fruit juice or canned vegetables but do not include potatoes.

Nutritional value

Fruits and vegetables are low in fat, except for avocado pears. Many fruits and vegetables are low in energy value and are good sources of NSP (dietary fibre). Citrus fruits and blackcurrants are rich sources of vitamin C, and yellow, red and orange fruits and vegetables supply the anti-oxidant pigment beta carotene (a form of vitamin A). Medical research suggests that the anti-oxidant vitamins A, C and E protect against certain diseases. We should therefore eat a wide variety of fruit and vegetables.

Healthier cooking

Some vitamins are destroyed by cooking and lost over time. Some minerals and vitamins may dissolve into cooking water. Tips on saving vitamins and minerals include:

- buy good quality fruit and vegetables and store in a cool, dark place for a short time
- buy fruit and vegetables when they are in season
- vitamins, minerals and NSP (dietary fibre) are often found just under the skin of fruit and vegetables; peel very thinly and use cleaned and unpeeled if possible
- cook vegetables quickly in a little water; steam or microwave if possible
- don't chop fruit and vegetables into small pieces – it exposes more of the surface and means more nutrients are lost
- prepare fruit and vegetables just before you need them – vitamin C is destroyed by warmth and time
- try to eat raw fruit and vegetables
- don't leave vegetables to stand in water – vitamin C and the B group vitamins dissolve out and are lost.

Choosing varieties

Different varieties of apple or potato have special cooking and eating properties. When manufacturers choose a potato to make into crisps, they specify the variety. The potato must have a low water content (a high dry matter content) to help reduce the amount of oil absorbed in frying. Potatoes for crisps also need a low glucose level to give the crisps a golden yellow colour when cooked.

Fruit and vegetables are nutritious but they also have functional properties. They can be used to give dishes colour, texture and flavour.

What types can you choose?

Fruits are processed in a variety of ways. Fresh fruit needs to be prepared and is best eaten when in season. You can select the individual fruits that you want to use.

Canned fruit and frozen fruit are easily available and ready prepared. They are good value for money and the pack usually contains similar sized pieces of fruit, which is useful if you want to decorate tarts and desserts.

If you were making fruit tartlets, which type of fruit would you choose – fresh, dried, canned or frozen?

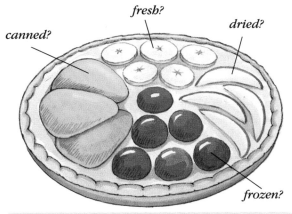

canned? *fresh?* *dried?* *frozen?*

Which type of fruit would you use for a fruit tartlet?

Changes during preparation

When you cut the surface of fresh fruit such as apples, pears and bananas, the cut surface can turn brown. The enzymes in the fruit react with the oxygen in the air in a process called enzymic browning. You need to add an acid such as lemon juice or sugar to the cut surface to prevent this change.

Beans, pulses, nuts and seeds

Beans, pulses, nuts and seeds are good sources of protein and NSP (dietary fibre) as well as carbohydrate, B group vitamins and some iron. Many seeds such as peanuts and sunflower seeds are rich sources of fat and are used to make vegetable oils for cooking.

Cooking beans

Beans and pulses are often dried and need to be soaked before they can be cooked. Some beans, including red and black kidney beans, contain toxins in their outer skin and must be boiled vigorously for 15 minutes to destroy these toxins.

Beans and pulses are used for products including dhal, made with lentils, chilli-con-carne, made with red kidney beans, baked beans, made from navy beans, and hummus from chickpeas.

Preserving fruit and vegetables

Fruit and vegetables can be preserved by the following methods:

- fruit such as strawberries can be made into jam
- vegetables such as peas and beans can be frozen
- fruit and vegetables such as peaches and carrots can be canned
- fruit and vegetables can be dried
- vegetables can be made into chutneys.

Questions

1 Why is it important to eat five portions of fruit and vegetables a day?

2 What is the nutritional value of fruits and vegetables in our diet?

3 How can you reduce loss of nutrients when preparing and cooking vegetables?

4 List five tips you could give to a soup manufacturer to help them improve the nutritional value of their vegetable soup.

Key points

- We should eat five portions of fruit and vegetables a day.
- Fruit and vegetables provide us with vitamin C, betacarotenes, carbohydrate and NSP (dietary fibre).
- Vegetables and fruit need careful preparation to avoid loss of vitamins and minerals.

Meat, poultry and fish

 TRF p.52

5.2.1a, c, d

Meat

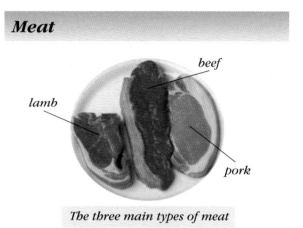

The three main types of meat

Beef, pork and lamb are the three main types of meat eaten in the UK. There are many popular meat products including beefburgers, sausages, meat pies and cook-chill meals.

Nutritional value of meat

Lean meat is a good source of high quality protein, iron and B group vitamins, especially vitamin B12. For healthy eating we should choose lower-fat versions of meat and poultry – this means cutting fat off chops and removing fatty parts such as the skin from chicken.

Why is meat cooked?

- to kill bacteria and make the meat safe to eat
- to make it tender and easier to eat
- to improve its flavour.

Meat can be cooked:

- by dry heat – by grilling, roasting, baking or frying
- in a liquid – by stewing, boiling, pressure cooking or casseroling.

Most bacteria are destroyed by heat, so meat and poultry must be thoroughly cooked to an inner temperature of 70°C or above.

Meat storage

Cooked meat must be kept separately from raw meat to avoid cross-contamination. Raw and cooked meat should be kept cool in the refrigerator. Raw meat needs to be stored at the bottom of the refrigerator so that the juices do not drip onto other foods. Minced meat must be eaten or cooked thoroughly on the day of purchase because it deteriorates quickly. Meat can be made more tender by mixing it with other ingredients in a marinade, and also by beating, chopping or mincing it.

Structure of meat

Meat is made up of muscle with connective tissue, fat and gristle. Muscle is made up of bundles of fibres which are bound together with connective tissue called collagen. The picture shows the muscle fibres lengthways and in cross-section.

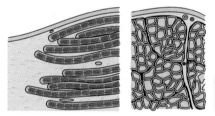

Muscles fibres

The tenderness of a cut of meat depends upon the amount and type of connective tissue, the length and thickness of the muscle fibres and the amount of fat within the muscle.

Poultry

Poultry includes chicken, duck and turkey. Chicken is a white meat and is becoming more popular as people choose to eat less red meat. Chicken is good value for money, and can be cooked and made into many products. There is a wide range of chicken cuts and products available, including portioned chicken such as drumsticks, breasts and products such as chicken Kiev.

Poultry contains as much protein as meat, but is lower in fat and more tender. It also provides B group vitamins.

Chicken and Salmonella

Much of the chicken sold in the UK contains the food poisoning bacteria *Salmonella*. Care is needed when handling and cooking chicken to avoid cross-contamination from one food to another. Chicken must be thoroughly cooked to a high enough temperature to kill off any *Salmonella* that might be present.

Meals with chicken

Chicken can be processed into products such as ready-cooked chicken, ready-meals (including roast chicken, pies, Chinese sweet and sour chicken, curries, tandoori chicken, chicken bites and nuggets), chicken spread and paté. Poultry is developed into many products because:

● it is inexpensive and popular

● white meat is encouraged by nutritionists

● it can be made into a wide range of products to save time.

Fish

Fish can be divided into three groups:

● white fish – cod, haddock, plaice, skate

● oily fish – herring, mackerel, salmon

● shellfish – crab, lobster, mussels.

Products made from white fish

● Cod is made into fish fingers, fish cakes, frozen fish in white sauce, fisherman's pie, goujons, dried salt cod, fish bits and cod in batter.

● Oily fish, such as tuna, is made into ready-meals such as tuna and pasta bake, tuna pat, tuna canned in oil or salt water, and sandwiches with tinned tuna.

Nutritional value of fish

Fish is a good source of protein and also contains the B group vitamins, and minerals such as iodine and fluoride. Fish that is eaten with the bones, such as canned salmon and tuna, is a good source of calcium. White fish like cod and plaice have very little fat in the flesh, as it is stored in their livers. Oily fish, such as mackerel and salmon, store fat in their flesh. Eating plenty of oily fish may reduce the risk of heart disease since the oil is rich in omega-3 fatty acids, which seem to reduce the risk of blood clotting.

White fish	*80% water*
	18% protein
	1% fat
	1% minerals
Oily fish	*68% water*
	19% protein
	15% fat
	2% minerals
Shellfish (edible part only)	*9% water*
	15% protein
	4% fat
	1% minerals

Cooking Fish

Fish cooks quickly. It can be cooked by steaming, poaching, frying, baking or microwaving. Fish cooks more quickly than meat or poultry as it contains less connective tissue.

Questions

1 Why is it important to cook meat properly?

2 How should raw meat be stored?

3 Why are some cuts of meat tougher than others?

4 Why must poultry be thoroughly cooked?

5 Why is poultry a popular ingredient for ready-meals?

6 What is the nutritional value of white and oily fish?

Key points

● Meat, poultry and fish are important sources of protein.

● They are made into a wide range of products and ready-meals.

Fats and oils

Types of fat include butter, margarine, cooking oils and reduced or low fat spreads. Fats and oils provide mainly fat but some also contain vitamins and essential fatty acids. Dietary guidelines recommend that fat should provide no more than 35% of food energy. We should eat less fat in our diet. Lower fat varieties of margarine can be used for spreading.

Various types of fat and oil are available for cooking

- Butter is made from churning cream to remove the liquid buttermilk. Butter is high in saturates and should be used sparingly in a healthy diet. Reduced fat alternatives and concentrated cooking butters are available. Ghee is clarified, unsalted butter used for Indian cookery.

- Margarine is made from a range of animal and vegetable fats, which are hardened by the addition of hydrogen gas – a process called hydrogenation. This process makes the fat more saturated, which helps the product to keep longer. Margarine labels show 'hydrogenated fat' and margarines are usually coloured, flavoured and fortified with vitamins A and D:

- Oil is usually liquid at room temperature. The main oils used in cooking are groundnut, sunflower, corn, soya, rapeseed and olive oil. Oil is used for salad dressings and frying, baking and roasting.

- Reduced or low fat spreads contain 40–80% fat. This compares favourably with margarine and butter, which are over 80% fat. They have a higher water content so they are not suitable for frying, roasting or baking. They are called spreads instead of margarine since they do not meet the legal requirements for margarine.

- Other fats used in cooking include lard, dripping and suet.

Cooking with different fats

Butter is chosen for cooking because of its delicious taste but there are many fats that are designed for different uses in cooking. For example, you can use soft margarines to make cakes, biscuits and sauces by the all-in-one method. There is a range of hard block spreads, white fats and lard that have special properties to make them useful for frying and pastry making.

How certain fats are used in cooking

Butter and margarine	Reduced fat margarine/spread	Half-fat butter/ margarine/spread	Low fat/light spread
80–82% fat	60–62% fat	39–41% fat	less than 40% fat
Spreading ✓	Spreading ✓	Spreading ✓	Spreading ✓
Baking ✓	All-in-one cakes ✓	Sautéing ✓	
Shallow frying ✓	Sautéing ✓	Sauces ✓	
Pastry ✓	Shortcrust pastry ✓	Scones ✓	
Sauces ✓	Sauces ✓	Choux pastry ✓	
	Scones ✓		

Source: Sainsbury's leaflet, *Finding Your Way Round the Chiller Cabinet*

Fats in pastry, cake and biscuit making

Fats are used to shorten baked products such as biscuits and pastry by making them soft and crumbly. Fat is mixed with flour and some fat forms a protective coating around the flour protein. Less water can mix with the protein so less gluten is formed and the mixture is softer.

Trapping air

When fat is beaten with sugar, air bubbles are trapped in the mixture. The air expands during cooking and the mixture rises. This process is used for cake and biscuit making. The food industry often uses fats that are suitable for vegetarians, such as butter and margarine made from vegetable oils. This means their products will sell to a wider range of people.

Genetic modification of oils

Genetic modification is undertaken to transfer genes with a desirable characteristic from an organism of one species to an organism of another. The technique has been used for plant crops such as soya, maize and oilseed rape to improve disease resistance or increase tolerance to weedkillers used during cultivation. It has been found that GM crops such as soya and maize have not been segregated from traditional crops after harvesting, so it is not possible to say if the product is or is not GM. Within the EU, special labeling is required if DNA/protein arising from GM is present in a food, ingredient, additive or flavouring. Scientists are developing testing or dipsticks for GMO screening.

Some consumers are concerned about eating genetically modified food. Scientists can identify and modify a particular gene that makes up certain characteristics in food. Cooking oils may well be made from genetically modified oilseed crops, and these could be sold in the shops and also made into commercial food products.

In response to consumer concern retailers such as Iceland have reacted by not stocking any food products with genetically modified ingredients.

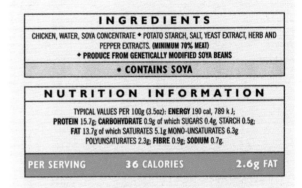

INGREDIENTS

CHICKEN, WATER, SOYA CONCENTRATE ✦ POTATO STARCH, SALT, YEAST EXTRACT, HERB AND PEPPER EXTRACTS. (MINIMUM 70% MEAT)
✦ PRODUCE FROM GENETICALLY MODIFIED SOYA BEANS

✦ **CONTAINS SOYA**

NUTRITION INFORMATION

TYPICAL VALUES PER 100g (3.5oz): **ENERGY** 190 cal, 789 k J;
PROTEIN 15.7g; **CARBOHYDRATE** 0.9g of which SUGARS 0.4g, STARCH 0.5g;
FAT 13.7g of which SATURATES 5.1g MONO-UNSATURATES 6.3g
POLYUNSATURATES 2.3g; **FIBRE** 0.9g; **SODIUM** 0.7g.

| PER SERVING | 36 CALORIES | 2.6g FAT |

This product contains genetically modified soya beans

Questions

1 Explain why you might want to change the fat in a product.

2 Which fat would you choose for the following products and processes? Give reasons for your answer:

   a making bread and butter pudding

   b frying onions and spices

   c making a salad dressing

   d spreading on bread for someone who is on a weight-reducing diet.

Key points

● Fats and oils have a wide range of uses in food products.

● There is a variety of fats available for different cooking methods.

Milk, cheese and dairy products

p.53

5.2.1a, c, d, f, 5.2.3b

Milk can be made into many types of products

Examples of milk and dairy products include milk, cheese, yogurt and fromage frais. The main nutrients found in dairy products are calcium, protein, vitamin B12 and vitamins A and D. For healthy eating, to lower the amount of fat in our diet, we should try lower fat versions such as semi-skimmed or skimmed milk, low fat yogurts or fromage frais and lower fat cheeses.

Milk and milk products

Most of the milk that we drink comes from cows, but we also drink milk from other animals such as goats and sheep. Soya milk is not strictly a milk since it is made from soya beans and does not come from animals. Soya milk is used by vegans to replace milk.

Nutritional value of milk

Milk is a good source of protein and calcium and also contains fat, carbohydrate and some B group vitamins, including B12. Whole milk also contains vitamin A.

Popular types of milk

- Whole milk – must have a minimum fat content of 3.5%.
- Homogenized milk – the cream is evenly mixed throughout the milk.
- Semi-skimmed milk – has about half the fat of whole milk and is suitable for anyone except children under the age of two.
- Skimmed milk – nearly all the fat has been removed to give this milk 0.1% fat. The milk looks and tastes less creamy than other milks.

Many people prefer to drink semi-skimmed and skimmed milk to lower the fat content of their diet. Semi-skimmed milk contains all the protein, minerals and most of the vitamins found in whole milk. Since skimmed milk has a low fat content, it contains less fat-soluble vitamins A and D than other milks.

Yogurt

To make yogurt, milk is heated, cooled and inoculated with a starter culture of bacteria. The yogurt thickens after being incubated at 40–45°C for 3–6 hours. This is due to the proteins coagulating. The yogurt is then cooled to 5°C for distribution and sale.

Cheese

Cheese is made by coagulating the protein in milk to make a curd and leaving a watery whey. The curd is then pressed to make hard cheese such as Cheddar. There are many types of cheese available, including vegetarian cheese made from vegetarian rennet. Cheese is a good source of protein and calcium.

Cooking changes in dairy products

Why does a skin form on the top of milk when it is heated?

Skin forms as milk is heated

Casein is the main protein in milk and this links with calcium in the milk and forms a skin when the milk is heated. Stirring the milk will prevent a skin forming.

Acid foods added to warm milk make the milk curdle

Why do milk sauces curdle?

When you add acid foods such as fruit juices, tomatoes or cheese to warm milk they make the casein coagulate and the milk curdles. To avoid this, mix the acid ingredient with flour or cornflour before adding to the milk.

Why does milk go sour?

After a few days the bacteria in milk turn the lactose (the milk sugar) into lactic acid. This makes the casein coagulate and curdles the milk.

Why does yogurt curdle when it is heated in sauces?

The thickness or viscosity of the yogurt is reduced when heated and the liquid seeps out leaving a curdled mixture. To avoid this, mix the yogurt with cornflour before cooking.

What happens to cheese when it is heated?

The fat in the cheese separates from the protein, and the cheese melts and spreads. The protein is denatured and if overcooked it can become tough and stringy. This is because the protein separates from the water and fat. As the cheese cooks it changes colour and becomes golden brown. Overcooking can turn it black as it decomposes. As the cheese cooks it gives out a delicious smell and the flavour changes. To cook cheese dishes successfully:

- heat them gently for a short time
- mix the cheese with starchy food such as breadcrumbs to absorb the fat
- grate the cheese so that it melts more easily.

Storing milk, cheese and dairy products

Milk, cheese and other dairy products should be stored in the refrigerator according to the 'use by' date on the food label. However, UHT milk can be kept at room temperature.

Questions

1 What is the nutritional value of dairy products?

2 List three products that can be made from each of the following:

   a milk   **b** yogurt   **c** cheese.

3 What happens to cheese on toast when it is cooked?

4 How would you avoid heated milk forming a skin?

5 If you wanted to make cheese sauce, how would you prevent it from curdling?

Key points

- Milk and dairy products are good sources of calcium and protein.
- To reduce fat content choose lower fat versions.

Eggs

pp.54–55

5.1.1b, 5.2.1a, c, d, e, f, 5.2.3b

Nutritional value of eggs

Eggs are made up of three parts – the shell, the white and the yolk. The yolk contains fat and is a rich source of cholesterol. Eggs provide minerals, iron, phosphorus and calcium. They also contain protein of a high nutritional value, fat and cholesterol and vitamin A. According to experts, eggs increase the level of good cholesterol, which can protect against heart disease.

Uses in cooking

When eggs are heated, the proteins coagulate. This property means that eggs have lots of uses in product design. For dishes such as custards and quiches, slow, even coagulation of the eggs is essential. Rapid cooking causes curdling.

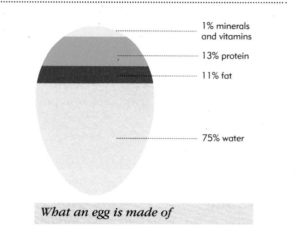

What an egg is made of

Whole eggs improve the flavour, texture and colour of dishes. The fat in eggs helps to shorten biscuits and cakes.

After purchase, eggs should be stored in the refrigerator and kept according to the 'use by' date on the food label.

The properties and uses of eggs

Property	How it works	What it is used for
Thickening	Coagulation of the egg protein thickens sauce. The dish must be cooked slowly to avoid overcooking and curdling.	Custards, quiches, soups.
Binding	The egg coagulates and sticks the dry ingredients together as they are cooking.	Used in bean burgers and rissoles, noodles and pasta.
Coating	Egg and breadcrumbs coat fish before frying. The egg coagulates and provides a strong coating which holds the product together. The coating helps to prevent oil seeping in during frying.	Used as a coating for fried fish, fish cakes and rissoles.
Forms a foam	Egg white can entrap air when it is beaten. The mixture sets when heated.	Used for Swiss roll and meringues.
Emulsifier	Eggs help to stabilize fat and sugar during cake making and to emulsify oil and vinegar when making mayonnaise.	Cakes and mayonnaise.
Glaze	During baking, the egg glaze turns golden brown.	Used to glaze pastries and pies.

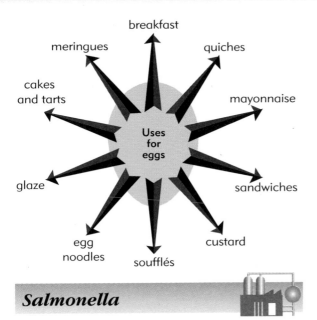

breakfast
meringues
quiches
cakes and tarts
mayonnaise
Uses for eggs
glaze
sandwiches
egg noodles
custard
soufflés

Salmonella

Raw eggs may contain the food poisoning bacteria *Salmonella*. To avoid outbreaks of food poisoning, many companies use pasteurized egg, which is heated to destroy *Salmonella*. This avoids the risk of cross-contamination from raw eggs and helps to make the food products safer. 74% of eggs sold in the UK show the Lion Quality mark on the egg shell and egg box. Lion Quality eggs come from hens that have been vaccinated against salmonella. All Lion Quality eggs are completely traceable and are packed, stored and transported under temperature controlled conditions which ensure quality and freshness. Lion Quality eggs are marked with a 'best before' date on the pack and on the eggs themselves 21 days after lay.

After purchase, eggs should be stored in the refrigerator and kept according to the 'use by' date on the food label.

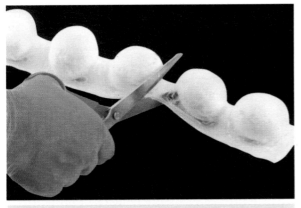

Pasteurized hard-boiled eggs for the food industry

The power of TV promotion

In 1998, Delia Smith's *How To Cook* programme showed viewers how to cook eggs and make omelettes. As a result of the programme, in six weeks, 54 million more eggs than average were eaten in Britain, which is enough to make 27 million omelettes, 13.5 million sponge cakes and 3 million gallons of custard.

Questions

1 What is the nutritional value of an egg?

2 What egg property is used in each of the following dishes:

   a egg quiche

   b Swiss roll

   c airy cakes

   d fried fish

   e egg noodles?

3 Why do eggs need careful handling for safety during food preparation?

4 Bread and butter pudding uses egg to set the custard. Explain why the pudding is cooked at a low temperature in the oven.

Key points

● Eggs have useful properties which can be used in different ways for food design.

● Eggs are nutritious.

● Eggs need careful handling to help improve food safety.

Sugar

Sugar is an important ingredient in many food products and also provides us with energy.

How is sugar made?

Sugar, in the form of sucrose, can be made from sugar beet or sugar cane. The beet or cane is crushed and mixed with water and the liquid boiled to obtain sugar crystals.

There are many ways that we eat sugar, including table sugar, sweets, preserves and sugary fizzy drinks. The main sugar used for cooking is made up of sucrose.

Different types of sugar

Choose the type of sugar that is suitable for the recipe. Fine icing sugar is used for icing cakes, caster sugar for baking and dark sugars give colour and flavour.

- Granulated sugar is used to sweeten tea and coffee and for sprinkling on breakfast cereals.
- Caster sugar is finer than granulated sugar and is used for cake and biscuit making.
- Icing sugar is a fine sugary powder and is used for icings and sweets.

Different varieties of sugars and syrup

- Brown sugars have a stronger flavour than white sugars and are used for gingerbreads and biscuits.

Functions of sugar in food preparation

These are some of the uses of sugar (sucrose) in food preparation:

- sugar makes food sweet
- in the right concentration, sugar preserves foods such as jams and chutneys
- sugar helps to change the flavour by removing the acidity of some products such as tomato ketchup
- dark sugars give colour and flavour to products such as cakes
- sugar acts as a bulking agent, giving texture to foods such as ice-cream and cakes – sugar is an inexpensive ingredient in food products
- sugar can speed up the fermentation process when yeast is used in breadmaking
- when sugar is beaten with butter or eggs it helps to make cakes light; when the sugar is whisked with egg whites for meringues it helps to keep the foam stable
- sugar can hold water and delay the drying and staling of baked products – it acts as a humectant.

What is invert sugar?

You will see 'invert sugar' listed on food labels for products such as sweets and chocolate products. Invert sugar is made commercially by hydrolyzing sucrose and splitting it into glucose and fructose. In some products – for example, some cakes – invert sugar has a humectant property and helps to keep the product moist.

Adapting the sugar in recipes

Reducing the amount of sugar in baked goods needs care. In cakes, biscuits and meringues the sugar helps to make the product light and forms part of the structure.

In jam making, the sugar and the pectin form a gel which makes the jam set. The correct balance between the ingredients is essential to make a successful, preserved product.

Cake with correct amount of sugar

Cake with reduced sugar

Cake with no sugar

The effects of changing the level of sugar in a cake recipe

Reducing the sugar in products: what are the choices?

If the sugar is used to sweeten the product you can look for alternatives such as fruit purées and artificial sweeteners. Check the function of the sugar in the product. If it helps to provide the structure and hold air, then you need to test the recipe carefully to make sure the adapted cake or biscuit will be successful.

Artificial sweeteners may change composition if they are heated. Check with the manufacturer's instructions. Recipe books can suggest ideas.

Questions

1   What is the function of sugar in the following products:

   a   strawberry jam   b   tomato ketchup

   c   fruit cake   d   meringues

   e   scones?

2   What problems might you face if you try to reduce the amount of sugar in some products?

3   The ingredients list for Smiley Faces Cakes is shown below.

   a   Which ingredients are sugar-based?

   b   Choose five of these ingredients and explain their function in the food product.

Ingredients: sugar, glucose syrup, wheat flour, animal and vegetable oils, water, milk chocolate beans, egg, whole milk powder, flavourings, invert sugar syrup, raising agents, modified starch, whey powder, cocoa powder, dextrose, glycerine, colours, stabilizers, sweetener, emulsifiers, salt, citric acid, gelling agent, gelatine.

Key points

● Sugar has a variety of functions in food products.

● Changing the amount of sugar in a recipe needs care.

Sugar comes in many forms

Sucrose	Maltose	Maple syrup	Invert sugar
hydrolyzed starch	golden syrup	glucose	dextrose
honey	lactose	fructose	treacle
glucose syrup	brown sugar	fruit juices	

Source: Health Education Authority, *Scientific Basis for Dental Health Education*, 4th edition, 1996

Cooking choices

 pp.56, 57, 58

5.1.6e, 5.1.7a

Food is cooked in many ways to make it tasty and also safer and easier to eat. When you are designing a food product, you need to decide how it will be cooked.

Cooking with water

Cooking methods that need water or other liquids include:

- boiling – foods such as vegetables are boiled in water in a saucepan
- simmering – foods that need more gentle cooking (e.g. eggs) are cooked slowly in liquids
- steaming – food is cooked in steamers over boiling water; this is a popular method for Chinese cooking

Boiling

Cooking with fat

Frying

Fats such as vegetable oils and butter are used to fry food and add flavour during the cooking process. Fat cooks the food at a higher temperature than water, so food cooks more quickly and often becomes crispy. Frying increases the energy value of the food.

- Shallow frying – food is cooked in very little fat. This method is used for fried eggs and sausages.
- Deep fat frying – foods are cooked in plenty of very hot fat. This method is used in fish and chip shops. Delicate foods such as fish need to be protected with batter.

- Dry frying – this method uses no fat at all. The food itself contains a little fat and it is best to use a non-stick pan for this method. Foods that can be dry-fried include bacon and sausages.

Cooking in the oven

- Roasting – this method involves basting the food with fat during cooking to improve the flavour. Meat, chicken and potatoes are traditionally roasted in the oven.
- Baking – foods are cooked on their own in an oven. Baked foods include baked potatoes, cakes, breads and fish.

Roasting

Other methods of cooking

- Grilling – food is cooked under the grill, which is a quick method of cooking by radiant heat. Food that can be grilled includes burgers, fish and toast.

Grilling

- Microwave cooking – this is a quick and economical method of cooking or reheating food. Food that can be microwaved includes ready meals, fish, vegetables and soup.

Methods of heat transfer

There are three ways that heat energy can be passed to food.

- Conduction – heat is conducted from molecule to molecule in solid or liquid food.

Metals conduct heat easily, which is why cooking pans are made from metals. Wood and plastic are poor conductors of heat and so these are used for stirring spoons and handles. Water is a good conductor of heat, which is why boiled food cooks more quickly than baked.

- Convection – heat travels around liquids and air by convection currents. Hot air rises and cool air falls, so ovens are hotter at the top. Baking and boiling are cooking methods that make use of convection currents.

- Radiation – food that is grilled or toasted is cooked by radiation so that the direct rays from the grill heat the food.

Most food is cooked by a combination of methods of heat transfer. Baked potatoes are cooked first by convection currents and then the heat is conducted through the potato to cook it.

How heat energy is transferred into food

Method of cooking	How the heat energy transfers to the food
Boiling	Heat is conducted through the pan to the liquid and convection currents pass the heat around to the food.
Steaming	Steam rises around the food by convection currents and the heat is then conducted through the food.
Frying	Heat is conducted through the pan to the fat and convection currents pass the heat around to the food; it is then conducted through the food.
Roasting and baking	Heat passes around the oven by convection currents and it is then conducted into the food.
Grilling	The grill gives off heat by radiation which passes to the food and is conducted through the food.
Microwave cooking	Microwaves are reflected off the metal walls of the cooker and are transmitted and absorbed by the food. The microwave energy is absorbed by the food, the molecules start to vibrate and this creates heat which cooks the food.

Cooking chicken in four minutes

Scientists have created a turbo-charged oven which can roast a chicken in four minutes. This process normally takes at least an hour. The TurboChef is fifteen times faster than the conventional oven and five times faster than a microwave. It uses a combination of microwave energy and jets of hot air which are heated and blasted onto the food below. Air is sucked around the food making it brown and crisp. At the same time the microwave energy cooks from within. Vegetables can be cooked in 100 seconds and pizza in 75 seconds.

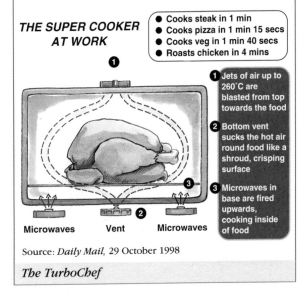

THE SUPER COOKER AT WORK

- Cooks steak in 1 min
- Cooks pizza in 1 min 15 secs
- Cooks veg in 1 min 40 secs
- Roasts chicken in 4 mins

1. Jets of air up to 260°C are blasted from top towards the food
2. Bottom vent sucks the hot air round food like a shroud, crisping surface
3. Microwaves in base are fired upwards, cooking inside of food

Microwaves   Vent   Microwaves

Source: *Daily Mail*, 29 October 1998

The TurboChef

Questions

1. Describe five methods of cooking that you could use to cook potatoes. How would the cooking methods affect the outcome?

2. Describe how the heat energy passes into a baked potato cooked in an oven.

Key points

- There is a variety of cooking methods used in food preparation.

- Large-scale manufacturers carry out the same processes but on a large scale.

Raising agents and setting ingredients

Raising agents are added to sweet and savoury mixtures to make them rise. There are three types of raising agent:

● air

● steam

● carbon dioxide gas.

How does a raising agent work?

The raising agent produces bubbles of gas. In a hot oven or in a steamer, the gas expands and pushes up the surrounding mixture. Some of the gas escapes and some is trapped in the mixture as it cooks and sets.

bubbles of gas in a cake or bread mixture   *heat makes the bubbles expand, pushing up the mixture*

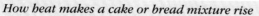

How heat makes a cake or bread mixture rise

Air can be introduced into mixtures when:

● flour is sieved for cakes and scones

● beating mixtures such as batters

● whisking egg whites to make meringues

● creaming fat and sugar to make cakes

● rubbing fat into flour for pastries and scones

● rolling and folding pastry such as flaky pastry.

Water changes to steam when it reaches boiling point. The steam escapes from the mixture, pushing it up, and the mixture sets on cooking. Steam is used as a raising agent in Yorkshire pudding, éclairs and some cakes and breads.

Carbon dioxide is produced in two ways in doughs for use as a raising agent.

1 Chemicals such as baking powder or bicarbonate of soda release carbon dioxide gas.

2 Yeast grows and ferments.

The carbon dioxide gas in the dough expands when heated and pushes up the surrounding mixture. The dough cooks and sets.

Chemical raising agents

● Baking powder is added to rich fruit cakes and scones. Baking powder is made from acid sodium pyrophosphate, rice flour and sodium bicarbonate, which react with the cake mixture and produce carbon dioxide gas.

● Bicarbonate of soda is used in gingerbread and chocolate cake and reacts with the cake mixture, releasing carbon dioxide gas.

● Yeast is a single-celled plant fungus which needs food, warmth and liquid to ferment. Most types of bread are made with yeast. The yeast uses the flour for food, and ferments with the liquid to produce carbon dioxide and alcohol. The dough increases in size during a process called 'proving' when the dough is left in a warm place, which encourages the yeast to grow. When the bread is baked, the carbon dioxide gas expands, pushing up the dough. The yeast is killed by the heat, the alcohol evaporates, and the bread dough cooks and sets.

Setting ingredients

Many savoury and sweet products use gelling agents to make them set. Gelling agents create a smooth, set texture in the product and help to suspend other foods in a jelly. You can use gelatine, starches such as cornflour and special vegetarian products to make dishes set.

Gelatine is made by boiling the bones and tissues from animal carcasses. The collagen in the connective tissue turns to gelatine when heated slowly in liquid. Gelatine is sold as a powder and in sheets, and is used to set jellies and mousses. It needs careful handling. Dissolve the gelatine in hot liquid, stirring gently. As the mixture cools, the mixture sets and thickens. If you use gelatine with a liquid with a high acid content, such as orange or lemon juice, you need to increase the amount used as the acid interferes with the gelling properties of the gelatine.

½ cup hot water or as required in recipe | Sprinkle gelatine into hot water. | Stir briskly until thoroughly mixed.

The instructions from a packet of gelatine powder

Vegetarian choices

Vegetarians and certain religious groups avoid gelatine as it comes from animals. Instead they use vegetarian alternatives to set products.

● Agar agar comes from a type of seaweed and is used to set milk and liquids with low acidity. Some fruits such as fresh pineapple, papaya and mango contain enzymes which break down the gelling action of agar agar. Acid fruits, such as oranges, need more agar agar to set the liquid. Powdered agar can be used in the same quantity as gelatine – about 2 teaspoons for 600 ml. Soak the agar in liquid, then boil and simmer until it dissolves.

● Carragheen is Irish moss. The food industry uses a by-product called carrageenan (E407) in ice-cream, jellies and frozen desserts. It acts as an emulsifying, thickening and gelling additive.

● Gelozone and Vege Geli are vegetarian setting ingredients that are made from a mixture of ingredients including carrageenan.

Pectin

Pectin is used to set jellies, marmalades and jams. Pectin is available as a liquid or powder and can be added to fruits during jam making to improve the setting quality. Pectin is found naturally in the cells of fruit and with the right proportion of acid and sugar will form a gel which helps the jam to set. When the jam is cool, the gelatine forms a network which sets and suspends the fruit, sugar and liquid. Jam manufacturers add commercial pectin, which is made from apples, to their jam to make sure that the jam sets.

Questions

1 How can air be introduced into mixtures?

2 Explain how chemical raising agents and yeast work in cake and bread mixtures.

3 Look at the food label below. What are the functions of the ingredients on the label? Give examples of foods that are set in different ways.

> **Ingredients:** blackcurrants, sugar, glucose syrup, gelling agent: pectin, citric acid, acidity regulator: sodium citrate. Total sugar content 63 g per 100g

This label for blackcurrant jam shows the use of pectin as the gelling agent

Key points

● Bubbles of gas expand when heated and make a food mixture rise.

● Many food products are set to make them firm and attractive to eat.

● Gelatine is not suitable for use in products for vegetarians.

Working with ingredients

pp.60–61

5.1.3e, 5.1.6b, c, d, e, 5.1.7d

Preparing food ingredients

You need to choose suitable equipment to prepare food ingredients efficiently and safely. On the small scale you may choose to prepare ingredients by hand or use small-scale equipment such as food processors and electric whisks.

When you are designing food products, test out the suitability of using the hand method compared with using machinery, to discover which method produces the best quality result.

Applying finishing methods

When a product has been prepared and cooked, finishing methods are often used to garnish or decorate the product, to make it look more attractive and appetizing.

Savoury foods can be garnished with chopped parsley or coriander, or slices of tomato which add colour and flavour to the dish. Sweet foods can be decorated with a dusting of icing sugar, swirls of piped cream or a sprinkling of chopped nuts.

Alternative ways of carrying out processes – by hand or by machine

Process	Hand method	Using machinery
Cutting, peeling, chopping	using a range of knives or jam tart cutters	the chopping blade in the food processor will chop food finely, and the slicing blade slices food such as potatoes or cucumber
Mixing in an appropriate way	mixing doughs and pastry by hand in a mixing bowl	using the processor to mix the dough in one process
Shape food ingredients	using tools to cut melon balls, gingerbread shapes, meatball shapers	you can use a food processor attachment to make sausages
Grating	using a Mouli grater or hand grater to grate cheese	a food processor has a grating attachment
Whisking	use a rotary whisk or balloon whisk to beat egg white	an electric whisk can beat egg whites quickly
Making pasta	roll and cut the pasta	use a machine to extrude the dough into strips

A food processor is useful if you have a lot of vegetables to prepare

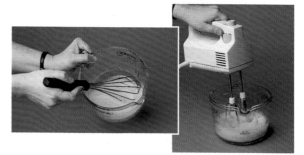

An electric whisk does the job in half the time

In food design it is important to understand the relevance of the function and aesthetics. The function is the purpose of the product and aesthetics concerns the looks, taste and attractiveness of the product.

Portion control

A portion is the amount of food that satisfies the needs of one person, but the weight of a portion can vary. When a food product, such a ready-meal, is packed, the nutrition information on the label shows the calculations for a portion or serving size. The book *Food Portion Sizes* (MAFF) provides typical weights for portion sizes of a range of foodstuffs. These are some typical portions:

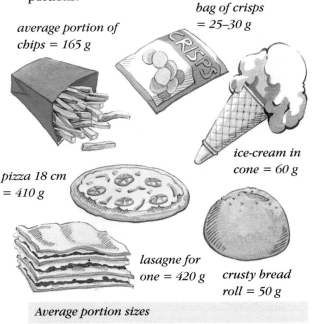

average portion of chips = 165 g

bag of crisps = 25–30 g

ice-cream in cone = 60 g

pizza 18 cm = 410 g

lasagne for one = 420 g

crusty bread roll = 50 g

Average portion sizes

Cooking instructions

You will see a range of cooking instructions on food labels. The products may be able to be cooked in a conventional oven or in a microwave oven.

Microwave cooking

Microwave cooking instructions can be found on food packs and show the time the product will take to cook in relation to the power output of the cooker. The lower power microwave ovens, such as those with an output of 650 watts, cook food slower than those with a high power output of 800 watts.

the microwave symbol — | the power output (watts) | 800W | the heating category for small packs | D

This label is for an 800-watt microwave oven

If you are cooking ready-meals in a conventional oven check the instructions to see which shelf should be used for cooking. In a conventional oven, convection currents circulate around and the hottest air moves to the top.

In fan-assisted ovens, the convection currents are disturbed as the fan moves the hot air around. There are normally special cooking instructions for these ovens on the food label.

Questions

1 List the equipment suitable to prepare the following products. In each case give examples of the equipment you would need if you were to prepare the food by hand *and* alternative electrical equipment you could use:

   a making shortcrust pastry

   b preparing vegetables for soup

   c cooking and making a smooth soup

   d preparing eggs to make meringues.

2 How would you decorate the following products for serving:

   a tomato soup

   b quiche

   c lemon mousse

   d fairy cakes?

   Give reasons for your choices.

3 Why are the instructions for a fan-assisted oven different from a conventional oven?

Key points

● Choose equipment appropriate to the task.
● The food label needs information on portion control and cooking instructions.

Ingredients in large-scale production

The ingredients used in large-scale manufacture have to meet the **product specification.** These ingredients are often different to those you can buy in the shops. Cake makers use special soft flours and fats that are good emulsifiers in the mixture. If you are considering scaling up a recipe, and comparing a kitchen recipe with one for a similar product sold in the shops, be aware that different qualities of ingredients will be used for the mass-produced version. If you were designing a large-scale recipe, you need to consider the use of **additives** which perform different functions in the recipe. Most of these additives are not available for kitchen recipes.

Additives

In the UK, there are over 300 listed additives and more than 3000 flavourings. Many prepared foods contain additives that are used to help food keep safe longer, to stop oils and fats from going rancid and to add colour to food. The 300 listed additives fall into three groups:

1 natural – made from natural products such as paprika and beetroot juice

2 nature identical – made to the same chemical formula as those extracted from natural products; for example, caramel used for colouring

The Ministry of Agriculture, Fisheries and Food produces useful consumer information, such as this booklet about food additives

Source: reproduced by permission of MAFF. © Crown copyright

3 artificial – made entirely from chemicals; for example, saccharin used to sweeten foods.

An 'E' number shows that the additive has been accepted as safe by the countries of the European Union.

Functions of additives

Additives have a range of functions. They are used as preservatives, antioxidants, colours, emulsifiers and stabilizers, flavour enhancers and sweeteners.

● Preservatives help to keep food safe for longer by protecting against the growth of micro-organisms. Processed food with a long shelf life often contains preservatives unless it has been preserved by another method such as freezing, canning or drying. This means that food can be transported and the storage time is increased. Preservatives include E200 (sorbic acid), which is used for soft drinks and fruit yogurt.

● Antioxidants prolong shelf life, stop fatty food from going rancid and protect fat-soluble vitamins from combining with oxygen. Antioxidants are used in dried soups, cheese spreads and sausages. Ascorbic acid (vitamin C) is a natural antioxidant that is found in fruit and prevents other fruits going brown – this is why lemon juice is added to peeled apples.

● Colours are added to food to make it look more attractive and to replace the colour that might be lost during processing. During canning, peas and strawberries both turn brown, so colouring can make them look more attractive. Caramel (E150) is the most popular colouring used for gravy powder, soft drinks and sauces. Many food colours used today come from, or are copied from, plant sources such as beetroot red (E162).

Emulsifiers and stabilizers allow fats and oils to mix with water to make low fat spreads and salad dressings. They give food a smooth and creamy texture, and help to improve the shelf life of baked goods. Lecithin, found in eggs, is a natural emulsifier used for mayonnaise and for low fat spreads.

Flavourings are used to restore flavours lost in processing and to add flavours to foods such as vanilla ice-cream. A flavour may be classified as natural, nature identical or artificial.

There are two types of sweetener.

1 Intense sweeteners (artificial sweeteners), such as saccharin, aspartame and acesulfame-K, are many times sweeter than sugar and only a little is needed. These intense sweeteners are used for low-calorie drinks and reduced sugar products.

2 Bulk sweeteners, such as hydrogenated glucose syrup, are used in the same sort of quantities as sugar.

Other additives include these.

Raising agents, such as sodium bicarbonate, are used to give a lighter texture to baked products.

Anti-caking agents, such as calcium silicate, which stop crystals and powders like salt and cocoa from sticking together.

Flour improvers, such as ascorbic acid (E300), which help to make bread dough stronger and more elastic.

Thickening agents, which are used to form a gel to thicken sauces.

Nutrients, such as vitamins and minerals, which are used to enrich certain foods (e.g. breakfast cereals) and to replace nutrients lost during processing.

Modified starch

Modified starch is an example of a modern food material (see page 12). It is often found on the list of ingredients for food products and is used to thicken soups, hot drinks and sauces.

It is made by chemically changing (modifying) a starch so that it will behave in the same way in a recipe every time. A food producer can then make a product to the same quality and standard each time. Other starch products, such as wheat, can change with climate conditions and storage.

INGREDIENTS
Full Cream Milk, Skimmed Milk, Sugar, Modified Starch, Flavouring, Colours: Curcumin, Annatto.

This canned custard uses modified starch

Questions

1 Describe the types of additive that might be used in a food product to:

a help the food keep longer

b make processed food more attractive

c help keep low fat spreads stable

d replace sugar as a sweetener.

2 What is the difference between natural, nature identical and artificial additives?

3 List the additives used on this cake label and give reasons for their use.

> **Ingredients:** sugar, water, wheat flour, fat reduced cocoa powder, pasteurized egg, glucose, hydrogenated vegetable fat, emulsifiers (E322, E471, E470, E435), skimmed milk powder, whey powder, maize starch, propylene glycol, sorbitol, stabilizer (guar gum E412), citric acid, vanillin.

4 What other ingredients on this label are not available for use in the home?

Key points

- The food industry uses specialist ingredients and may use additives in food products.

- There are a large number of food additives, each with a particular function.

Components of foods

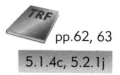 pp.62, 63

5.1.4c, 5.2.1j

Components are the parts that make up a product. For example:

- durum wheat is made into flour, which is a component of pasta
- pasta is a component in a spaghetti Bolognese, and so also is the tomato sauce
- pastry is a component in apple pie and Cornish pasties
- a ready-made pie filling can be a component for a fruit pie.

The food industry

In the food industry, manufacturers buy in standard components. These are the ingredients or parts of the recipe that come ready prepared. The standard component must contain the same ingredients to the same standard every time, so that manufacturers can guarantee the quality of the end product.

Examples of components used by the food industry include: stock cubes, pre-mixed seasonings, ready-to-use flavourings such as fruit purées, raising agents such as baking powder, chopped herbs, ready-prepared and canned fruit and vegetables, ready-made pizza bases and pastry, processed sauces, ready grated cheese, cooked eggs, fondant icing and decorations for icing cakes.

Pizza
*cheese arrives ready grated
tomato paste is pre-mixed
pizza base is bought in*

Cake
*fondant icing is
ready made
marzipan is bought
ready prepared*

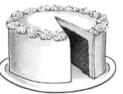

Rice, peas and prawns
*peas arrive processed and frozen
prawns are ready cooked and frozen*

The components for three food products

What are the advantages and disadvantages of using components?

Advantages	Disadvantages
Saves preparation time	You rely upon a manufacturer to supply the product so their problems become yours
Saves staff skill, costs and equipment	The taste and quality may not be as good as using your own ingredients
You get the same results every time	Other food companies may use the same components
The quality is guaranteed	The components may be expensive
You are getting the components from experts who know how to make them	
It saves relying on several suppliers to provide the separate ingredients	
It can make food preparation safer because the high-risk processes – such as vegetable preparation that needs soil removal – are carried out in another place	
If egg products are cooked elsewhere, this removes the risk of contamination from raw egg	

Using components in a product

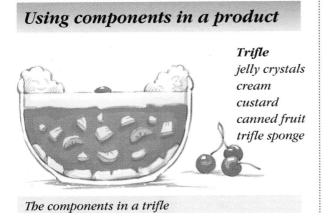

Trifle
jelly crystals
cream
custard
canned fruit
trifle sponge

The components in a trifle

This trifle uses several components to make the product:

- the jelly is made with ready-made jelly crystals
- the cream comes ready squeezed from an aerosol can
- the sponge cakes are ready cooked
- the fruit is ready-to-use in the can
- the custard is ready prepared.

Components used in apple pie production

Manor Bakeries is the largest cake manufacturer in the UK. They make Mr Kipling, Cadbury's and Lyons cakes. The photo shows the production of Mr Kipling pies.

Production of Mr Kipling pies at Manor Bakeries

Mr Kipling apple pies are made from pastry with an apple filling. The company uses ready-peeled and chopped apples which are coated in natural preservative to prevent browning. The pastry is made from raw ingredients in a huge mixer then squeezed and moulded into the shape of the pie base. The filling of apples and sugar is added and the top is pressed on to the pie and sealed. Notice the special apple shape on the top of the pie and the 'thumbnails' to seal the edges. The pies are baked for eight minutes in a travelling oven, sprinkled with sugar then cooled and taken to the packing area ready for distribution. The pies have a shelf life of 28 days.

A Mr Kipling apple pie

Questions

1 How could you make the following products using components:

   a a fruit pie

   b vegetable soup

   c lasagne?

2 For each of these products explain the advantages and disadvantages of using components.

3 Explain why the factory uses some ready prepared ingredients for the apple pies.

Key points

- Components are used by the food industry to save preparation time and costs.
- Components help to produce a product that looks and tastes the same every time.

Making quality food products

If you want to cook and present food products that look, measure and weigh roughly the same each time, there is a range of small-scale equipment that can help you to keep the quality you need.

Ingredients in recipes must be weighed accurately to get the results you expect. Electronic scales can weigh small amounts of ingredients from 5 grams in weight.

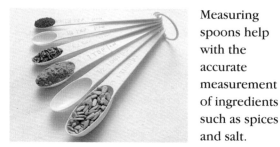

Measuring spoons help with the accurate measurement of ingredients such as spices and salt.

If products are cooked in the oven, you need to be sure that the oven is working at the correct temperature and that the products are cooked for the same amount of time. An oven thermometer and digital timer can help you to check these details.

Hexagonal scone cutters can cut a whole sheet of biscuits or scones in one go without any waste. In industry, large cutting machinery is used for this process.

Muffin pans are deep enough to hold the soft muffin mixture, and the paper cases help to prevent the baked muffins from sticking to the pan.

A non-stick, heavy-duty fluted loaf pan helps to make sponge cakes and breads that are the same size and shape.

For many years, shortbread has been pressed into special shortbread moulds with patterns and divisions to make the shortbread easy to share into portions.

This apple segmenter is similar to one used in the mass preparation of apples by the catering and airline industries.

The apple segments are cut to exactly the same size and shape each time.

In industry, large-scale equipment is used to make food products such as ice cream and yogurt. You can get an idea of small-scale production by trying machines such as a yogurt maker, an ice-creamer and a popcorn maker.

How does the food industry maintain quality?

The food industry sets up quality systems to maintain standards throughout production. Large-scale equipment has been developed to help **quality control.** Automatic weighing machines help with weighing portions of products for packaging, such as this machine to check and weigh snack products.

Machinery can cut potatoes into straight and crinkle-cut fries and potato dices that are the same shape and size.

Questions

1 Give two reasons:

   a why people sometimes like to have products the same size and shape every time

   b why the food industry wants similar food products made on a large scale to look and weigh the same every time they are made.

2 Make a list of the small-scale equipment shown on these pages that could help you to:

   a keep your products the same size and shape each time they are made

   b maintain your standards of accuracy and measurement

   c copy on a small scale a food making process usually carried out on a larger scale.

3 From your own research, describe how machinery is used to help control the quality, size and shape of a food product made on a large scale.

Key points

● Food products often need to be made the same size and shape.

● Small- and large-scale equipment can help maintain quality standards.

Preservation

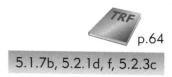
Why does preservation stop food going bad?

Bacteria, yeasts and mould cause changes in food which can be harmful. Micro-organisms need food, warmth, moisture and time to multiply. If these conditions are removed the food is preserved and will keep for a long time. Enzymes in food also cause deterioration and these enzymes must be destroyed to improve the keeping quality of food. Food is preserved in many ways so that it keeps longer.

Chemicals used for preservation

- Salt (sodium chloride) is used to salt meat and fish.
- Sodium nitrate and nitrite are used to make bacon from pork.
- Sugar is used to preserve fruits and make jams and jellies.
- Vinegar is used to preserve vegetables to make pickles and chutneys.
- Alcohol is used for fruits such as peaches in brandy.
- Smoke is a way of preserving fish and meat – e.g. smoked salmon.
- Spices are used to preserve meats – e.g. salami.

How do chemicals work?

Chemicals remove the available water from food so that micro-organisms cannot multiply.

Drying (dehydration)

Micro-organisms need water to grow and multiply. Drying (dehydration) is a very old method of preservation in which much of the water is removed from food. For example, grapes are dried to make sultanas and raisins. Many fruits such as apricots and figs are dried.

Accelerated Freeze Drying (AFD)

For this process, food is frozen and dried under vacuum. The ice changes to water vapour without passing through the liquid stage. This process preserves the flavour and colour of the food, and is used for soups and instant coffee granules.

Nutrition and keeping times

Dried foods have a higher energy value than fresh foods because of the loss of water. Vitamin C is lost during drying.

Dried foods, such as prunes and sultanas, have a different taste to the fresh version but they can be eaten out of season. They occupy less space than fresh foods and keep for a long time.

Dried food such as pasta and rice keeps for about twelve months and dried fruits about six months, at ambient temperature (i.e. room temperature). Store dried foods in a cool, dry place.

Chilling and freezing

If food is kept chilled, micro-organisms do not multiply as quickly as at room temperature. Chilled food is kept at below 8°C. There are many chilled products such as ready-meals and cooked meats for sale in chiller compartments.

Freezing

Food can be stored for a long time by freezing it. Micro-organisms become inactive at around −10°C and enzymes are inactive at −18°C. Domestic freezers, used in the home, should operate at −18°C or below and commercial freezers used by canteens or supermarkets should operate at −29°C.

Why does freezing preserve food?

Freezing turns water into ice. Micro-organisms need food, warmth, liquid (moisture) and time to multiply. Freezing removes the warmth and liquid.

How is food frozen?

Factories where food is frozen use three different methods of freezing:

- plate freezing – flat products such as beefburgers and fish are frozen on plates
- **blast freezing** – cold air is blasted over food such as vegetables
- cryogenic freezing or immersion freezing – the food passes through a tunnel and is immersed or sprayed with liquid nitrogen or carbon dioxide. The food is frozen immediately but this is an expensive process.

Notes on freezing

Before freezing vegetables it is important to blanch them by dipping them in boiling water to stop enzymes working, and to prevent browning and loss of vitamins.

Follow the packet instructions for frozen food and make sure the freezer is operating at −18°C or below.

Nutritional loss

The nutritional loss in frozen foods is very small. Blanching causes some loss of the water-soluble vitamins C and thiamin but the final cooking time is reduced, so frozen vegetables can be just as nutritious as fresh. Many frozen vegetables are more nutritious than the fresh version since they are frozen very quickly after harvesting.

Canning

Food is placed in a can, the liquid added, the can sealed, and the can and contents heated until harmful micro-organisms and spores are killed. Canned vegetables and meat are usually heated to 115°C and fruits to a lower temperature.

High Temperature Short Time canning (HTST)

Very high temperatures reduce processing time and prevent food from becoming over-processed and losing texture.

Nutritional loss

Some loss of nutrients occurs during heating. Thiamin is lost from meat and vitamin C from fruit and vegetables. However, canned foods are nearly as good as their fresh equivalent in nutritional value. Fruit and vegetables are canned within hours of picking so few nutrients are lost.

Store undamaged cans in a cool, dry place. Check the 'best before' date.

A variety of methods is used to preserve food products

Questions

1 What chemicals are used to preserve food and how do they work as preservatives?

2 Describe the different methods of drying food.

3 Why does chilling and freezing food help it to keep longer?

4 What are the nutritional losses from frozen and canned food?

5 How does canning preserve food?

Key points

- Food is preserved to keep it longer.
- Micro-organisms need food, warmth and moisture to multiply.

Preservation and cook-chill

Pasteurization

Heat treatment can lengthen shelf life and make a product safer to eat. For milk, pasteurization involves heating to 72°C, holding for at least 15 seconds and cooling rapidly to 10°C. Pasteurization destroys many but not all of the micro-organisms present.

Sterilization

This involves heating food to a high temperature. Milk is heated to 104°C for 40 minutes.

UHT (Ultra Heat Treatment)

This process destroys all bacteria. Milk is heated to 132–140°C for up to 5 seconds and cooled quickly. This makes the milk sterile but alters the taste. UHT milk will keep for several months without refrigeration.

Irradiation

Food is irradiated by bombarding it with ionizing radiation to make it keep longer. Irradiation reduces or eliminates harmful micro-organisms, kills insects, delays the ripening of fruit and prevents sprouting of vegetables. This method of preservation is permitted in the UK and irradiated food must, by law, be labelled as such.

MAP (Modified Atmosphere Packaging)

This is a method of keeping food longer by altering the atmosphere around the food so that it is different to air. Once fruit, vegetables, fish or meat have been harvested or slaughtered, changes take place that alter the colour, flavour and texture.

In **MAP,** the products are packed in combinations of carbon dioxide, nitrogen and oxygen gas, which increase the shelf life of the products.

Vacuum packing

Vacuum packing removes all or most of the air from the package and keeps food in anaerobic conditions with no oxygen so the food will keep for a long time. The diagram below shows how the products are vacuum packed and sealed for distribution.

1. *Fill the pouch or pouches and place in the evacuation chamber.*

2. *Close the lid and the sequence of operations automatically begin.*

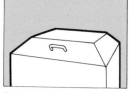

3. *A built-in pump can achieve a 99.9% vacuum and then seals the pouch using a heat impulse.*

4. *Air returns to the chamber, the lid opens and your pack or packs can safely be removed.*

This vacuum packing machine can handle single packs or several at once

Cook-chill foods

Ready-to-eat chilled or frozen meals are kept in chiller or freezer cabinets in supermarkets. Popular chilled meals include shepherds' pie, curries, Chinese sweet and sour dishes and chilli-con-carne. Ready-to-eat meals can also be frozen.

Cook-chill and **cook-freeze** products must be hygienically and safely prepared. Cook-chill foods are fully cooked, fast chilled, then stored at low temperatures above freezing point (0°C to 3°C).

The process of making a cook-chill product, with control checks

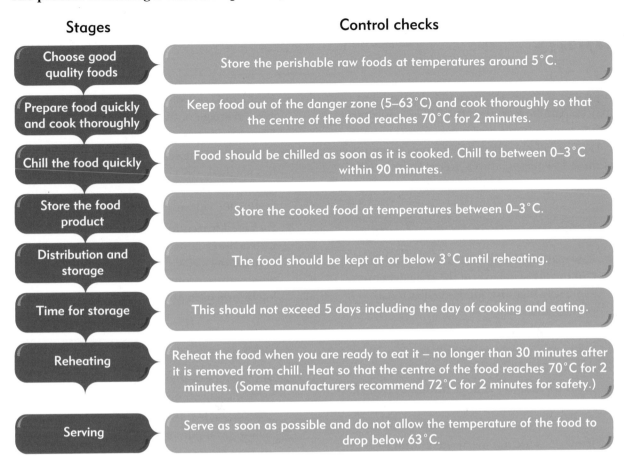

Stages — Control checks

Stages	Control checks
Choose good quality foods	Store the perishable raw foods at temperatures around 5°C.
Prepare food quickly and cook thoroughly	Keep food out of the danger zone (5–63°C) and cook thoroughly so that the centre of the food reaches 70°C for 2 minutes.
Chill the food quickly	Food should be chilled as soon as it is cooked. Chill to between 0–3°C within 90 minutes.
Store the food product	Store the cooked food at temperatures between 0–3°C.
Distribution and storage	The food should be kept at or below 3°C until reheating.
Time for storage	This should not exceed 5 days including the day of cooking and eating.
Reheating	Reheat the food when you are ready to eat it – no longer than 30 minutes after it is removed from chill. Heat so that the centre of the food reaches 70°C for 2 minutes. (Some manufacturers recommend 72°C for 2 minutes for safety.)
Serving	Serve as soon as possible and do not allow the temperature of the food to drop below 63°C.

They can be used for up to five days, which includes the day of cooking and the day of eating. The food must not be eaten after this time as the quality and safety decreases.

If food products are kept chilled, the bacteria become inactive and do not multiply rapidly, which prolongs the shelf life of the product.

Cook-chill products are sometimes packed in a modified atmosphere, which extends the shelf life.

Key points

- New methods of preservation include MAP and irradiation.
- Cook-chill meals should be stored at 0–3°C for no more than five days.

Questions

1 Explain what is meant by the terms:
   a UHT
   b irradiation
   c MAP
   d cook-chill.

2 Temperature control is essential throughout the production of a cook-chill product. Explain which steps in the process of making to eating require careful temperature control.

3 Imagine that you are making a cook-chill meal such as sweet and sour pork with rice. List the stages in the process from making to storage in the shops, and explain what control checks you would use for each stage.

Cook-freeze foods

5.1.7b, c, 5.2.1f, 5.2.2b, 5.2.3c, 5.2.4d, 5.2.5c

Cook-freeze foods are often fully cooked, but may be part cooked, then fast frozen and stored at low temperatures well below freezing point (−18°C or below). Micro-organisms cannot grow at these low temperatures, so the foods can be stored for several months if frozen.

Facts about frozen products

- Raw materials must meet the microbiological and quality standards of the specification, especially high-risk foods such as meat, poultry and fish.

- Freezing does not destroy any microbial toxins that may have formed, but it reduces the activity of micro-organisms.

- Flavours of spices change during freezing and storage so food should be tasted during product design to take this into account.

- If enzymes are not inactivated during blanching, they can damage the flavour and texture of food.

- A sensory evaluation is needed during product development to test the flavour and texture of the product after freezing and thawing, and to identify any unwanted changes.

- Raw materials should be prepared in a separate area from the cooking, blanching and production of the finished product, to avoid cross-contamination.

- Preparation rooms should be kept at 8°C and have air filters to remove any micro-organisms.

- **Critical control points** in the process must be monitored and recorded on graphs for future records.

- Products that have been heated during preparation should be cooled quickly to below 8°C.

- Rapid and controlled freezing is needed to avoid damage of the cells by the growth of large ice crystals.

- Freezing is complete when the thermal centre has reached −18°C and the temperature should not rise above −18°C during packing and palletization.

- Packaged frozen foods must carry storage instructions. Long-term stores should be kept at or below −26°C. Thermometers and temperature probes are needed to check and log information at least every 24 hours.

Questions

1 If you were designing a frozen product, why would you need to freeze and thaw the product as part of your trialling?

2 What are the important temperature checks needed during the preparation, freezing and storage of a frozen product?

3 How is the temperature monitored and recorded?

4 Why do raw materials have to be prepared in a separate area from the rest of the process?

Key points

- Frozen food needs special temperature controls during processing.
- Hygiene is very important to ensure a safe product.

Questions

Pasta product design

You want to make a pasta dish with a sauce. The pasta gives bulk, texture and colour and provides lots of carbohydrate. The sauce gives flavour, moistness and colour to the dish. You can come up with recipe ideas by changing the type of pasta and the sauce. Pasta choices include:

- different shapes
- different colours
- made from white or wholemeal durum wheat.

Sauce choices include:

- colour – red sauces are made from tomatoes, yellow sauces from cheese and cream
- moistness is provided by liquid from tomatoes, water and milk
- flavour – add tomatoes and tomato paste, or different varieties of cheese.

1 Create a pasta dish with a sauce. Give details of the pasta chosen and the sauce. Explain why you have chosen these types of pasta and sauce.

2 If you had to make changes to the recipe, how would you alter the ingredients?

Crisps – preparation and cooking

The way you prepare ingredients can affect the finished product. The table shows the fat content in 100 grams of different potato crisps. The potatoes have been cut in different ways to make them thin, thick or crinkle cut. When they are fried in oil the thinner crisps with the largest surface area absorb the most fat.

3 Which type of crisp contains:

   a the least fat

   b the most fat?

4 Explain why the fat content changes.

5 Why do you think crisp companies manufacture a range of crisps?

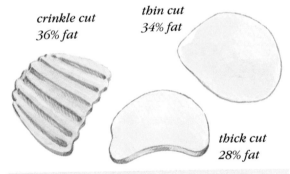

crinkle cut 36% fat

thin cut 34% fat

thick cut 28% fat

Different types of crisp

The composition of various types of crisp per 100 g

	Energy value kcal	Energy value kJ	Fat g	Carbohydrate g
Potato crisps	530	2215	34.2	53.3
Crinkle cut	547	2282	35.8	53.9
Jacket	510	2128	32.4	51.3
Low-fat	458	1924	21.5	63.5
Square	433	1816	21.2	57.7
Thick-cut	499	2090	28.1	58.0
Thick, crinkle-cut	507	2119	30.3	55.9

Source: McCance and Widdowson, *Composition of Food*

Chilled and frozen products

6 What is the difference between cook-chill and cook-freeze food products?

7 This label from a spicy chicken ready meal shows the cooking instructions for the oven and for the microwave. Explain:

a why the sleeve must be removed and the film lid pierced

b why the dish should be cooked in the middle of the oven

c the difference in the cooking times between the chilled and frozen product

d why a non-metallic plate must be used in the microwave oven

e why the product must be piping hot and what this means?

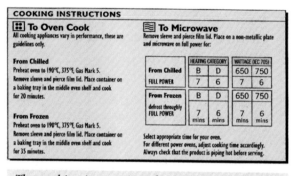

COOKING INSTRUCTIONS

To Oven Cook
All cooking appliances vary in performance, these are guidelines only.

From Chilled
Preheat oven to 190°C, 375°F, Gas Mark 5.
Remove sleeve and pierce film lid. Place container on a baking tray in the middle oven shelf and cook for 20 minutes.

From Frozen
Preheat oven to 190°C, 375°F, Gas Mark 5.
Remove sleeve and pierce film lid. Place container on a baking tray in the middle oven shelf and cook for 35 minutes.

To Microwave
Remove sleeve and pierce film lid. Place on a non-metallic plate and microwave on full power for:

	HEATING CATEGORY		WATTAGE (IEC 705)	
From Chilled	B	D	650	750
FULL POWER	7	6	7	6
From Frozen	B	D	650	750
defrost throughly FULL POWER	7 mins	6 mins	7 mins	6 mins

Select appropriate time for your oven.
For different power ovens, adjust cooking time accordingly.
Always check that the product is piping hot before serving.

The cooking instructions for Sainsbury's Chicken Peri Peri

8 Use the food facts listed below to help explain why meat, poultry and fish have been developed into such a wide range of ready-meals.

> **Food facts**
> - Demand for microwavable products is increasing.
> - Canned food is becoming more exciting.
> - People want more variety of choice including ethnic food.
> - People want food to be more convenient.
> - More single portions are needed.
> - People want healthy food.

9 Look at the chart showing the new chilled food products produced in 1997. What is meant by the terms:

a ready-meal

b added value

c deli-type products

d accompaniments

e dressings?

New chilled food products for 1999

Product group	Number of new food products
Meat, poultry, fish, vegetable and meat alternatives, ready-meals, recipes dishes and added value products, including snack ready-meals	921
Vegetables, salads, pasta and rice	324
Sandwiches and hot-eat sandwich alternatives (burger style)	328
Desserts	362
Pies and pastries (meat, poultry, fish, vegetable and meat alternatives)	172
Deli-type products (cooked/ ready-to-eat meats, dips and paté)	307
Dairy products (cheese and spreads)	208
Yogurts and fromage frais	113
Pizzas and savoury breads	127
Accompaniments, dressings, marinades	95
Meat, poultry, fish, sausages	88
Savoury and cooking sauces	72
Soups	95

Source: Campden and Chorleywood New Products 1999

10 Give examples of canned, frozen and chilled food products made from meat, chicken and fish. Complete a chart like the one below.

Canned food	Frozen	Chilled

FOOD PRODUCTION

The design process

5.1.2b, c, f, 5.1.4c, 5.1.7c, 5.1.9a, c, d

These are the stages that might be taken by a food product design team when creating a new product. The development of a product up until the launch can take about three months.

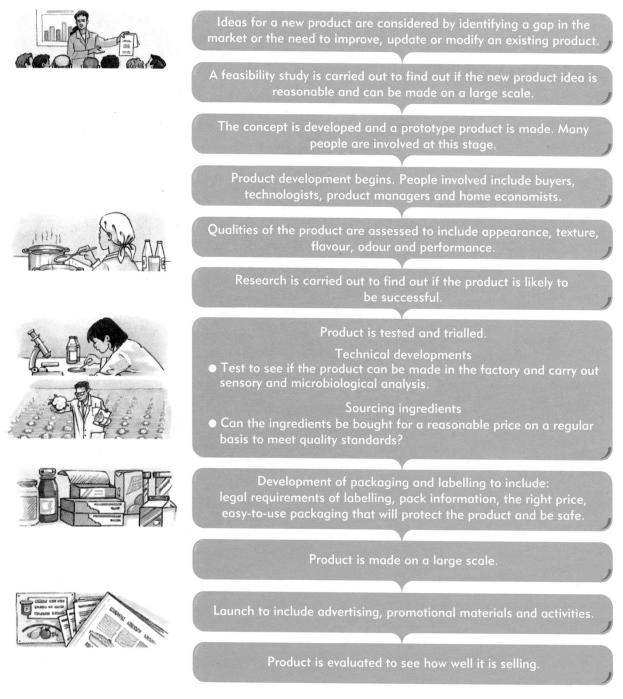

Ideas for a new product are considered by identifying a gap in the market or the need to improve, update or modify an existing product.

A feasibility study is carried out to find out if the new product idea is reasonable and can be made on a large scale.

The concept is developed and a prototype product is made. Many people are involved at this stage.

Product development begins. People involved include buyers, technologists, product managers and home economists.

Qualities of the product are assessed to include appearance, texture, flavour, odour and performance.

Research is carried out to find out if the product is likely to be successful.

Product is tested and trialled.

Technical developments
● Test to see if the product can be made in the factory and carry out sensory and microbiological analysis.

Sourcing ingredients
● Can the ingredients be bought for a reasonable price on a regular basis to meet quality standards?

Development of packaging and labelling to include:
legal requirements of labelling, pack information, the right price, easy-to-use packaging that will protect the product and be safe.

Product is made on a large scale.

Launch to include advertising, promotional materials and activities.

Product is evaluated to see how well it is selling.

This chart is based on a concept developed by Sally Hookham, The Food Business

Jobs in the food industry

Many people are involved in designing and making a food product. The size of the food factory affects the number of people involved in the product development team. A small company may ask for experts to work as consultants for small sections of the project. For example, a designer can work on recipes and specifications.

These are some of the job descriptions for people in an industry team.

- General manager – in charge of everything.
- Product development technologist – makes sure that the specification details are correctly produced and followed.
- Production manager – in charge of planning the time for production.
- Quality control manager – sets up **quality assurance** procedures, and is responsible for checking product quality, process control and making sure the product meets legal requirements and codes of practice.
- Health and safety manager – makes sure that people are trained and follow hygienic and safe procedures, looks after equipment safety and maintenance and follows legal requirements. Sets up **HACCP** system (see page 86).
- Product buyer – finds where to buy ingredients for product, likely costs and availability.
- Food technologist – knows about the equipment needed, the science of the ingredients, legal implications. The food technologist can be called the technical manager, responsible for production methods.
- Packaging technologist – decides on the type of packaging to be used.
- Nutritionists – examine nutritional content.
- Production line supervisor – makes sure that people are working efficiently and that the machinery is operating effectively.

Simulation of a product run

You may need to test whether your product can be made in quantity. One way is to carry out a classroom simulation of large-scale production.

Ask several students to work in a team and form a production line for your product. Work out the stages of production and the different tasks for the team members. Test out your ideas with a trial run. Think about how you will maintain quality and hygiene standards during production. Evaluate the outcome.

A classroom simulation of large-scale production

Questions

1 Describe, in two sentences, the design process for developing a new food product, based on the information shown in the chart on the opposite page.

2 Think of three new food products that you have seen promoted on the television, radio or in supermarkets recently. Explain why you think that food producers may have decided to develop each of these food products. Do you think they will all be successful? Give reasons for your answers.

3 If you ran a small food company, make a list of people that you would like to have in your team. Provide a job description for each one.

Key points

- The development of a product can take three months and follows a process.
- The food industry uses teams of people for product design.

Marketing and advertising

5.1.1c, 5.1.2a, d, 5.1.8h, 5.1.9c, 5.2.1i

Before developing a new product, the food industry carries out research to find out if the product will be marketable and sell. Researchers need to find out if the new product is a good idea before too much money is spent on development.

What is marketing?

Marketing is used to find out the demand for goods and services and to discover how to encourage people to buy them. A product should be designed to meet a need. Products include food products, kitchen equipment, motor cars – goods that we buy.

When a new product is being developed for sale, the designers need to consider:

- *what* the consumer wants to buy – the market trends
- *why* they will want to buy it – is it cheap, attractive, convenient?
- *when* they buy it – a snack food could be bought on the move
- *where* they buy it – snack foods could be bought from garages or newsagents
- *who* will buy it – snack foods may appeal to teenagers.

Large businesses have marketing departments whose role is to keep track of market trends, to find out what people need and want to buy, and to make sure the goods and services they are offering are meeting the demand and standards required.

Marketing a product

There are four main factors to consider when marketing a product. These are known as the four Ps.

1 *Product* – is the product what people need or want?

2 *Price* – is it sold at the price that people are willing to pay?

3 *Place* – is it sold in the right place, where people will go to buy it?

4 *Promotion* – is it promoted effectively by advertising, special offers or displays?

Market research is used to help businesses plan how they will promote and advertise a product and to find out if there is a need for a product. Here are some questions that could be asked:

- Is there a market for the product?
- How much might people pay for it?
- Can the product be made economically?
- Is there a need for technical development and expenditure to make the product?
- Can the product be distributed and sold efficiently?

Many large companies use consumer research to find out people's views throughout the development of a new product. They often employ special agencies to carry out this research. There are different ways of carrying out market research:

- direct research from the public by telephone, personal and group interviews, tasting and testing sessions, questionnaires
- secondary research using existing information such as reports like *Social Trends*, computer **databases** and CD-ROMs.

This CD-ROM is useful for secondary research about new food products

Research can be quantitative (using questionnaires and interviews) or qualitative (asking small groups of people for their opinions on products). A group usually consists of less than ten people, and the interviewer finds out their likes and dislikes for certain products and how the product could be improved to be more appealing.

Market-place intelligence

Companies wanting to develop a new product can get a lot of information by watching what is happening in supermarkets, by watching television and by using information from the food research associations. Competitors may be launching a new range of products that suggest changes in market trends. These trends could be for a healthier food product, ethnic foods or new forms of packaging. Market intelligence can be gained by visiting stores and finding out what is happening, and by watching television advertisements.

The product life cycle

This is the period of time that the product remains popular and in demand. Some products, such as chocolate bars, have a long life cycle and the recipe is not changed very often – although the product still needs to be promoted. New products need to be promoted and at first the sales will be slow. If people like the product, the sales will grow quickly. After a time, the sales of many products slow down and the product is eventually withdrawn. Food companies may redesign the product to boost sales. They may change the recipe, alter the taste or create new packaging and special offers.

The product life cycle

Advertising food products

As the product is being developed, an advertising department is working out ways to promote and advertise the product ready for sale. Over £600 million is spent every year on advertising food.

The biggest advertising spenders include chocolate, crisps, snacks and sweet manufacturers.

Advertising brings us information about products and services and aims to give us reasons to buy things. Most new products need to be advertised so that people know they are available.

Advertisements should target the group most likely to buy the product and give them information they might need. Advertisements are found on TV and radio, in newspapers and magazines, at the cinema and on posters. Where a product will be advertised depends upon the target audience (what they read, watch or listen to) and the advertising budget for the project.

Other ways to promote a product

These include special offers, gifts, competitions, and leaflet distribution to homes and in the streets.

'Below the line' advertising includes direct mail, competitions, sponsorship, in-store tastings, point-of-sale advertising and door-to-door drops.

Marketing terms
- A market trend is the way people buy things.
- A market profile of a product describes the type of people who buy a product. For example, frozen pizzas may be bought by families with teenage children.

Questions
1 Why is market research important before a new product is developed?
2 How is market research carried out?
3 What is meant by a product life cycle?
4 Why is advertising important for a new product?

Key points
- Industry carries out careful market research before launching a new product.
- Products have a life cycle.
- Advertising and promotion are essential for a food product to succeed.

Production methods

pp.65–69, 70, 71, 72

5.1.8a, 5.1.9a, 5.2.4b

If a company wants to make large quantities of a food product, it needs a system for mass production. Large-scale machinery is used for the stages in the process and the system is often computer-controlled to maintain the quality at each stage. This machinery is often specially designed for the task – for example, pasta machines that can make different shapes of pasta. For efficiency, this machinery needs to be checked regularly to make sure that no parts are broken. Problems could result if pieces of machinery fell into the food products!

Some methods of mass production include: batch production, continual flow process (also known as 'continuous flow'), job production (also known as 'one-off', 'jobbing', or 'craft production') and repetitive flow (also known as 'assembly line').

Continual flow process

Some products can be made twenty-four hours a day for seven days a week. The factory or plant stops for cleaning the machinery and workspace, but the process of making the product can continue non-stop.

Products that can be made by continuous flow include crisps, breakfast cereals, soft drinks, margarines and spreads. Raw material processing that is carried out by continuous flow includes making flour from wheat, pasteurizing raw milk and making refined sugar. These processes are computer controlled to produce a high quality product. Only a small workforce is needed to maintain the process.

Batch production

This method is used to make products such as cakes, biscuits and breads. Products are made in batches when a specific amount, for example 300 cakes, is needed for distribution. If too many are made then the product could be wasted. The production line can usually be adapted to make other types of cake or biscuit. So one batch of muffins may be made from chocolate chips, then the machinery will be thoroughly cleaned so that the next batch can be made from blueberries. The photos opposite show batch production of bread.

Job production

This process is used when a customer wants only one product. Examples include wedding and birthday cakes, iced chocolate eggs and food designed for special occasions.

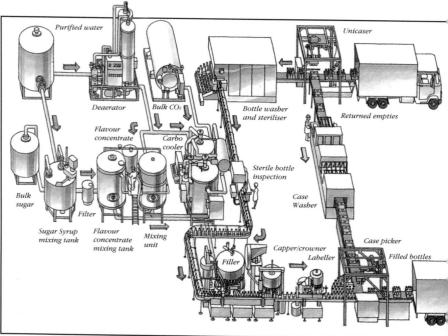

A soft drinks factory like this can run continuously, 24 hours a day

Repetitive flow

This involves producing large numbers of identical products at a low cost. Production is broken down into smaller sub-assemblies of smaller components. For example, in sandwich production the bread, fillings and packaging would be dealt with by different people on an assembly line, each repeating one individual task to contribute to the production of the finished sandwich. This form of mass production can be labour intensive or completely automated – depending on the product.

Process	Advantages	Disadvantages
Batch production	The company can make small orders and change the recipe each time. Machinery can be used for other products. If necessary, the plant can be shut down if the company is not busy.	Expensive to set up and maintain. Must keep up to date with competitors. May need lots of skilled staff to produce product. Expensive to train and pay staff.
Continual flow process	Inexpensive to run. Requires few staff.	Expensive to set up and maintain. Dedicated to one process. Quality maintenance essential.
Job production	A unique product for a special occasion.	Hand crafted, so expensive and cannot be mass produced.
Repetitive flow	Large numbers of identical products can be produced to fulfil orders quickly.	Can be labour intensive. Expensive to pay and train staff.

A batch of dough is tipped into a hopper

The dough is cut into accurately weighed portions

The dough is pressed into tins ready for cooking in a travelling oven

Questions

1 Explain the difference between batch production and continual flow process. What are the advantages and disadvantages of each process?

2 Which method of production or process would you use for the following products:

a apple pies   b fizzy drinks

c canned beans   d bread rolls

e tomato soup   f margarine?

Give reasons for your answer.

Key points

- Batch production is used when a specific quantity of a certain product is needed.
- Continual flow process is used when the same product is made continually, non-stop for 24 hours a day.
- Job production is for products that are made specially for one occasion.
- Repetitive flow is used to mass produce indentical products on an assembly line.

81

Product specifications

The main purpose of a product specification is to make sure that the product can be made many times to the same standards every time. The product specification is usually the work of a product development technologist.

In the food industry the product specification may include:

- a list of raw materials with the suppliers
- the recipe or formulation
- methods of making
- process flow chart, including HACCP (see page 86) and safety checks
- critical control points
- analytical standards
- microbiological standards – the amount of bacteria acceptable in the product
- pack declarations, including nutrition information
- packaging specification
- shelf life details
- finished product weights and tolerances
- finished product sensory specification and tolerances
- customer instructions.

For example, the following information is from a bakery that makes small iced cakes. These are some of the specification details they have to give when they make a product for a client:

- product title
- product descriptor
- declared weight or size (average or minimum)
- **e mark**
- target weight size.

This is an example of an outline of the manufacturing process from a product specification:

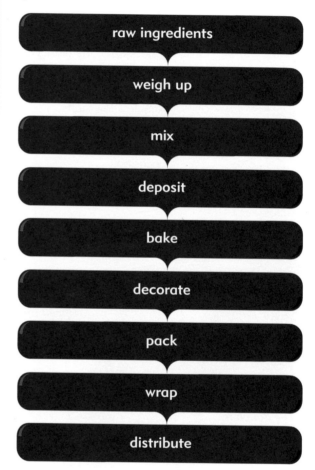

raw ingredients

weigh up

mix

deposit

bake

decorate

pack

wrap

distribute

The company also has to guarantee that the goods will be delivered undamaged, that the ingredients comply with the Food Safety Act 1990, and that the product is safe within the requirements of the General Product Safety Regulations 1994 and the safety provisions under the Consumer Protection Act 1987. The company must also guarantee that the premises where the product is made comply with the standards of cleanliness and hygiene required by the Food Safety Act.

To support the food label, customer dietary intolerance information is needed:

Description	Yes/No
Free from additives	
Free from azo colours	
Free from benzoates	
Free from BHA/BHT	
Free from egg/egg derivatives	
Free from genetic modification	
Free from glutamate	
Free from milk/milk derivatives	
Free from nuts and sesame seeds	
Free from shellfish	
Free from soya/soya derivatives	
Free from sulphur dioxide	
Suitable for halal requirements	
Suitable for vegetarians	
Suitable for vegans	
Free from wheat and wheat derivatives	
Genetically modified? If yes, give details:	

Further information is needed for product claims:

May contain traces of nuts or seeds	Packed in a protective atmosphere
No artificial flavourings	Soya free/GM soya free
Maize free/GM maize free	No added colours
No preservatives	

The specification provides details of the way the final product will look and taste:

- product description
- appearance after cooking if applicable
- cooking method
- aroma
- flavour
- texture
- visual description.

Tolerance

Tolerance levels are built into all specifications. The designated tolerance is the amount of flexibility allowed in a recipe or method so that the product can have the same standards of quality and sensory properties.

For example, when Patak fill pouches with Tarka Dhal, they allow a tolerance of plus or minus 5 g in the filling weight of 150 g. This is written 150 g $\pm$ 5 g. The tolerance level for commercially produced scones is written as standard raw scone 60 g $\pm$3 g, so the scone could weigh 63 g or 57 g and still pass the control checks. The critical dimensions of a product are its size and shape. For example, a fruit tart might be 5.5 cm in diameter and 2.5 cm in depth.

Questions

1 Why is a product specification important for manufacturers? Give three reasons for your answer.

2 What product details must be given for the small iced cakes before production begins?

3 What is meant by tolerance levels and critical dimensions?

Key points

- A product specification is essential to maintain quality and standards.
- The specification is very detailed.

Systems for food production

5.1.2f, 5.1.7c, 5.1.8a–c, 5.1.9d, 5.2.2a–c

A system is a collection of things that work together to perform a task. A system has three parts:

- input
- process
- output.

A recipe is a system with input (the raw materials), process (making the product) and output (the final product).

Cake making is a system. The input is the ingredients (flour, fat, sugar, eggs); the process is the making and baking; the output is the baked cake.

This is known as an open loop system with the system shown as input, process and output in a line.

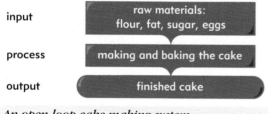

An open loop cake making system

Advantages of using a system for food production

- Stages in the process are planned and can be controlled.
- It helps to produce a good quality product.
- It saves time, money and mistakes.
- It saves wasting ingredients.

Feedback

Feedback is important in a system and is used by control systems to check that the output is correct. The information is fed back into the system and can be shown as a decision box in the flow diagram with a yes or no answer.

Feedback can include controls for weight and mix, temperature control, control by thermostats and sensors and control of shelf life and storage. If you are controlling the size of a loaf of bread, you can measure the volume as part of your system. If it does not meet the specification, the feedback would be to adapt the part of the system where the problem occurs.

Feedback when cooling cooked chicken

The warm chicken enters the chilling unit and is cooled to 2°C. If the chicken does not reach that temperature there will be serious food safety problems. The feedback checks the system to find out if the temperature controls are working and if the chicken has been cooled for enough time. If not, the system needs to be changed.

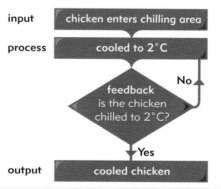

A system for cooling chickens, with a feedback control

Control systems

Time controls can be analogue or digital. Analogue time controls are in a continuous state of change and are the traditional method of controls. Digital controls are better because they can measure time very precisely and can be connected to computer systems. Speed and quality of systems can be controlled using switches, sensors and dials. Computer software is designed to create a system for a product.

This is how an oven thermostat works as a system control:

- the oven temperature is set and the oven heats up
- the thermostat is the sensor that controls the temperature
- the oven heats up until the correct temperature is reached
- the sensor monitors changes in the oven temperature and when the correct temperature has been reached, the sensor reduces the power input which is usually electricity or gas
- if the temperature falls below the temperature setting, the sensor turns up the heat so that the oven reaches the required temperature again.

This is called a closed loop system as the decision making relies on feedback. The diagram of the chicken cooling system is an example of a closed loop system.

Flour milling

Rank Hovis McDougall is one of the largest flour milling companies in the country. The flour mills process the wheat from grain to flour and the system is computer controlled. The photograph above shows the control room in a mill, with visual displays on the computer screens so that the manager can see exactly what is happening in each area.

The wheat grain is ground into white flour and the bran and germ are taken by pipes to different areas in the mill to be blended into flour products.

In the room in this photograph you see an electronically controlled chart which shows how the factory is working. This is known as a mimic panel and shows how the plant is working so that any problems can be dealt with immediately.

Large bakeries are run by computer systems to help them produce a range of different breads. This is often called computer-aided manufacture or **CAM**. All stages are controlled, including the amount of flour in the recipe, oven temperatures, cooling times and packing. Records are kept to show evidence of due diligence, which means that the manufacturers have taken all the steps necessary to prepare a product that is safe to eat.

Electronic sensors detect changes in food and relay this information back to the computer. If changes outside the specification have occurred then the process could be stopped until the problem has been solved. Sensors can test for:

- weight changes in the product as it is loaded into baking tins
- temperature changes in ovens, cooling or freezing units
- changes in colour in the product as it is cooked
- products that are not within the tolerance level for weight and dimensions
- the rate of flow, the pressure, the pH and the moisture content products.

Questions

1 What is a system and why are systems needed to control food production?

2 How can control systems help improve food production?

3 Why is feedback important in food systems?

Key points

- A system has input, process and output.
- A closed loop system has feedback.

Hazard Analysis and Critical Control Point

p.78

5.1.2b, 5.1.4c, 5.1.7c, 5.1.8c, 5.1.9d, 5.2.2b, c, 5.2.4b, d, 5.2.5b, d

The Hazard Analysis and Critical Control Point (HACCP) system was developed in the 1960s in the USA to prevent food safety problems occurring in food production. The Food Safety (General Food Hygiene) Regulations 1995 requires food businesses to assess the risks in making their food products and to take any required action to ensure the safety of the food.

- HACCP is an example of a system that identifies specific hazards and risks associated with food production and describes ways to control these hazards.
- HACCP identifies control points and critical control points in the making of a food product.
- HACCP is introduced when the product is being developed and is part of a quality assurance programme.

Hazards and risks

In food products, a hazard is anything that is likely to cause harm to a consumer. A hazard could be:

- biological – such as *Salmonella* in chicken
- chemical – such as cleaning chemicals in food
- physical – such as glass in food.

In food production, a risk is the likelihood of a hazard occurring.

What is a control point and a critical control point?

A control point is the step in the process where hazards are likely to occur.

A critical control point is a step that *must* be applied to prevent or reduce a food hazard. For example, if a meal is reheated, it is critical it reaches a temperature of 70°C for 2 minutes to destroy harmful bacteria.

Steps in setting up a simple HACCP system

- Draw a flow diagram to show the steps in the making process.
- Show any hazards that might happen at each step.
- Are the hazards high, medium or low risk?
- If the hazards are high risk, show that this is a critical control point.
- Suggest control checks for each step and at the critical control points.

What are high-risk foods?

These are foods that are often used without further cooking and easily support the growth of food poisoning organisms. High-risk foods include cooked chicken, mayonnaise, cooked ham, eggs and dairy products.

In a system such as HACCP, the control measures or checks are the methods of feedback to make sure that the system is working effectively.

Industry note

To avoid the risk of contamination by bacteria, a sandwich factory would use pasteurized mayonnaise and can even buy in pasteurized boiled eggs that are safe to use (see photo on page 53).

Using IT

In industry, HACCP systems can be constructed using computer programs. This HACCP software program has been developed for use in school and helps create flow charts for hazard analysis as well as showing interactive case studies.

The steps and hazard analysis for making a hard-boiled egg sandwich

	Process	Hazard	Risk level of hazard	Control measures	Critical control point?	Tests for control
1	Collect eggs	Eggs may contain *Salmonella*.	High risk.	Store eggs away from other ingredients. Reject cracked eggs.	Yes	Check refrigerator temperature is at or below 5°C. Handle eggs with care.
2	Collect sandwich ingredients	Ingredients may not be safe to eat.	Medium risk.	Keep chilled foods cold. Check datemark of ingredients and quality.	No	Check refrigerator temperature is at or below 5°C.
3	Boil the egg until hard, then cool in cold water	Eggs may contain *Salmonella*. Egg shells can cause physical contamination of sandwiches.	High risk.	Make sure the egg is boiled for 10 minutes.	Yes	Cook the egg for the correct temperature and time.
4	Mash the egg with bottled mayonnaise for the filling	Eggs and mayonnaise are high-risk foods.	High risk.	Mix quickly and store for a short time in cool conditions.	Yes	Check refrigerator temperature is at or below 5°C. Store for a limited time.
5	Make the sandwiches	Food handlers may not work hygienically.	High risk.	Train food handlers in good hygiene practices and make and store the sandwiches quickly.	Yes	Check food handlers for hygiene and safety. Keep preparation area cool and clean.
6	Store sandwiches for eating	Bacteria can multiply in warm temperatures and over time.	High risk.	Check that sandwiches are cool, clean and covered.	Yes	Store in refrigerator at or below 5°C for less than 4 hours.

Thank you to Rushmoor Borough Council environmental health officers for assistance in this work

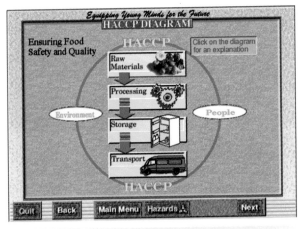

HACCP software specially developed for use in school

Questions

1 What is meant by HACCP and why is this system used by the food industry?

2 Draw up a simple HACCP system for the process of making one of the following products:

   a a loaf of bread   **b** an omelette.

Key points

● HACCP is an example of a system used by the food industry that identifies specific hazards and risks associated with food production.

● Hazards can be biological, chemical and physical.

Using larger equipment

Special equipment is designed for the food industry to help tackle the production processes efficiently and quickly.

Indian ready-meals

Noon Products Ltd makes chilled and frozen Indian ready-meals. The food is cooked by traditional methods to make sure the authentic flavours develop, but the equipment used is much larger than home cooking.

The company produces many types of chicken and rice dishes.

Cooking the chicken

The chicken is put on non-stick sheets before passing through the oven

The chicken pieces have been tossed in a sauce and are placed on a Teflon-coated sheet which is non-stick. The chicken passes through a temperature-controlled travelling oven, which cooks the chicken thoroughly to a high temperature. The Teflon-coated sheet is washed and reused. This avoids the use of baking sheets, which would be more difficult to clean. The food worker wears blue disposable gloves to avoid any contamination of the chicken.

Mixing the sauce

Tomatoes are a popular ingredient in Indian sauces so the tomatoes are made into a pulp with the blades of a large liquidizer.

Liquidizing tomatoes

Cooking the rice

Pilau rice in a Bratt pan

Pilau rice is made by frying spices and onion in oil then adding the rice and water. On the large scale, the rice is cooked in a Bratt pan, which is a wide, shallow pan that is usually made from stainless steel and heated by gas or electricity. The Bratt pan can be used for frying the spices and onion, and then the rice and water are added. Throughout this process, the chefs stir the pilau with a large paddle. Bratt pans are also used to boil the vegetables and fry chapatis.

Baking bread

An industrial dough mixer

In the baking industry, the ingredients are mixed in huge computer-controlled dough mixers. The dough then passes directly into a hopper and then on to a divider which cuts the dough into equally sized portions.

Bread is cooked in a long, travelling oven, cooled in a chill area and taken by conveyor belts for packaging, labelling and distribution. These large-scale processes

The bread passes through a large travelling oven

are examples of mechanized manufacture which makes sure that the product has the same consistency and quality every time. It also allows for longer work times without breaks.

Small-scale and large-scale processes compared

Small scale	Large scale
Weighing ingredients using scales	Computer controlled weighing or measured into hoppers
Slicing vegetables using a knife	Automatic slicer fed from hopper
Peeling potatoes with a peeler	Mechanical peelers with specially lined drum
Rolling out dough with a rolling pin	Dough is sheeted using rollers
Cutting dough with tart cutters	Dough is cut using rollers with blades
Puréeing in a liquidizer	Enormous liquidizer used
Cooking in a saucepan	Large Bratt pans used
Cooking in an oven	Computer-controlled travelling or tunnel ovens, or rotary ovens
Cooling on a wire rack	**Blast chilled** in cooling tunnels
Cutting dough into portions with knife	Automatic cutting
Portion controlled with spoon measure	Squeezed out with an extruder
Using a food probe for temperature control	Sensors are computer controlled
Mixing in a bowl or processor	Giant mixing systems used
Piping bag for cream	Injector or extruder
Piping bag for biscuits	Depositing machine

Robotics

Robotics is an activity carried out by computer-driven devices that imitate the activities that can be carried out by human beings. Robots are used to help make some food products but they are very expensive to design. They are used by the industry to fillet fish, bone chicken and pack chocolates. Robots can work non-stop, twenty-four hours a day, seven days a week, which saves time and money for industry.

This robot is packing biscuits

Questions

1 What sort of large-scale equipment do you think you would you need to make:

   a frozen part-fried chips from raw potatoes

   b pastry from raw ingredients

   c a batch of biscuits?

2 What are the advantages of using large-scale equipment?

Key points

- Large-scale equipment is specially designed for a particular task.
- The equipment may only be used for one type of food product or can be adapted to prepare several products.

Quality

Quality of design

Good design is essential for quality products. Quality of design is about creating a design that is easy to make, with a clear specification and production process. The product must meet the needs of the target group and, if well planned, may reduce costs and increase profits.

Quality of manufacture

When judging the quality of manufacture, you are looking at the way the products are made and how effective the quality checks are at each stage. Staff need special training in quality checking so that they know what they are looking for.

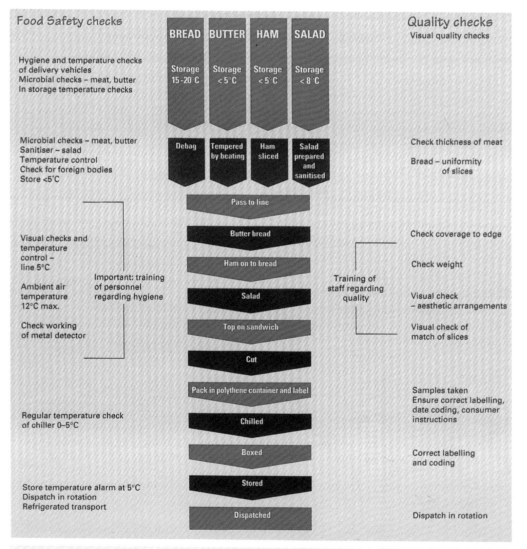

Safety and quality checks in ham sandwich manufacture

Source: Taken from 'The Meat in Your Sandwich' video-based learning pack, published by the Meat and Livestock Commission

Quality assurance

Quality assurance is a system that identifies in advance where problems are likely to occur and sets up control systems to stop them happening. Quality assurance includes hygiene procedures and quality control points, and the system makes sure that the end product is safe and meets quality standards.

Quality of raw ingredients

This diagram shows the process of packing frozen peas. The peas have already been sorted and graded for size, cleaned, blanched and frozen. After they have been checked to see that they are an acceptable colour, they are ready for packaging. At every stage, checks are made by people or with the use of computer-controlled machinery.

Quality of production

The chart opposite shows the production of a ham sandwich made from bread, butter, ham and salad. On one side are the food safety checks and on the other quality checks.

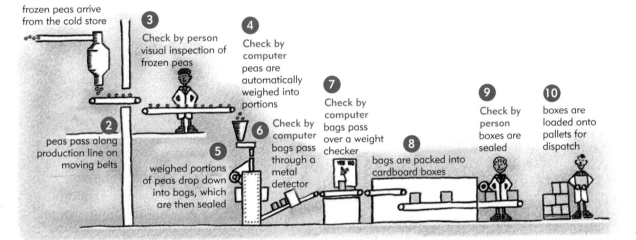

Packing frozen peas

Source: Birds Eye Wall's, *How do they do that?*

Questions

Use the diagram for the frozen peas to answer questions 1–3.

1 List the ten steps in the process of packing frozen peas.

2 For each step on your list, show where checks are carried out by people or using computer-controlled machinery.

3 Explain why people are needed for some of the check points.

Use the chart for ham sandwich manufacture to answer questions 4 and 5.

4 Make a list of the visual quality checks that are made during sandwich manufacture.

5 What steps in the making process need checking for weight and size?

Key points

● Quality assurance procedures are needed throughout production to ensure a good product.

● Everyone involved in the product from farm to factory is responsible for quality.

Scaling up for mass production

p.82

5.1.2b, 5.1.7c, 5.1.8a, c, 5.1.9a, 5.2.2a, b, 5.2.5c

Most food companies make a kitchen sample recipe to test out their design ideas. When the recipe has been trialled and is acceptable it needs to be scaled up for factory production. Often the large-scale recipe is in the same proportions as the kitchen sample.

This case study shows how Patak's have scaled up the recipe for Tarka Dhal, which is a lentil based dish with spices. To make the product on a large scale, it is heat treated to sterilize the spices and cook the lentils, and then frozen. The product can also be canned but needs to be prepared by a different method (see page 94).

Small kitchen recipe

This is the recipe for Tarka Dhal to serve two people. It is based on the industrial recipe. This is the kitchen method that would be used for making it on a small scale.

Please note: This is an industry specification, so the ingredients are listed in the recipe in order of weight, instead of in order of use.

This frozen Tarka Dhal is made from a scaled-up recipe

Ingredients

- 320 g hot water
- 200 g onions peeled
- 80 g red lentils
- 30 g rapeseed oil
- 15 g chopped fresh tomato
- 5 g salt
- 4 g sugar
- 2.5 g cumin seeds
- 2.5 g garlic powder
- 2 g ground cumin
- 2 g ground turmeric
- 0.1 g chilli powder

Kitchen method

1   Weigh all the ingredients.
2   Dice the onions to 4–5 mm.
3   Put the oil in a large pan and add the onions.
4   Stir and simmer gently for 15 minutes.
5   Remove from the heat and add the sugar, salt, spices and seeds and mix until the onions are coated. Add the hot water and the lentils.
6   Return the pan to the heat and bring to the boil, stirring continuously.
7   Lower the heat, cover with a lid and simmer for 25 minutes.
8   Stir occasionally and add more water if the mixture looks dry.
9   Add the chopped tomato towards the end.
10 If the mixture looks a little watery, remove the lid and simmer to evaporate some of the liquid.
11 Serve hot with bread and sprinkle on some chopped, fresh coriander (optional).

The scaled-up recipe

A large steam-heated cooking pan

This is the industrial method for the same product, made on a large scale. The onion is delivered ready diced and large cooking pans are used which contain automatic stirrers. The pan is heated with a steam jacket, which is a cost-effective method to transfer heat. It is easily controlled and does not burn the food.

Industrial method

1 Weigh the ingredients manually and add the oil and onions to the large cooking pan.

2 Cover and cook for 15 minutes – an automatic stirrer moves the food in the pan.

3 Add the spices and seasoning and measure in the water at 80°C. Add the lentils.

4 Cover and cook for 5 minutes at 105–110°C under pressure, to reduce the cooking time.

5 Add the chopped tomatoes at the end to avoid loss of colour and texture.

6 The mixture is ready to go into the hopper to fill the flexible pouches. The filling weight is controlled by computer and the mixture temperature must be greater than 65°C for safety.

7 The pouches are frozen to –26°C within 2 hours and packed in a cardboard sleeve.

8 For distribution the product is stored at –20°C in commercial freezers.

9 The dhal can be cooked from frozen and eaten as part of a meal, as a snack or with bread.

The industrial method is controlled during weighing and preparing and with such careful cooking there is no loss of water, so water adjustment at the end is not needed. The Tarka Dhal is cooked at 105–110°C because this cooks the product more quickly.

The critical control point is to make sure that the product does not fall below 65°C when it is filled into the pouches.

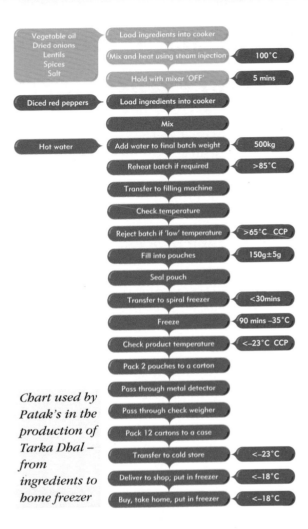

Chart used by Patak's in the production of Tarka Dhal – from ingredients to home freezer

Vegetable oil / Dried onions / Lentils / Spices / Salt → Load ingredients into cooker → Mix and heat using steam injection — 100°C → Hold with mixer 'OFF' — 5 mins

Diced red peppers → Load ingredients into cooker → Mix

Hot water → Add water to final batch weight — 500kg → Reheat batch if required — >85°C → Transfer to filling machine → Check temperature → Reject batch if 'low' temperature — >65°C CCP → Fill into pouches — 150g±5g → Seal pouch → Transfer to spiral freezer — <30mins → Freeze — 90 mins –35°C → Check product temperature — <–23°C CCP → Pack 2 pouches to a carton → Pass through metal detector → Pass through check weigher → Pack 12 cartons to a case → Transfer to cold store — <–23°C → Deliver to shop; put in freezer — <–18°C → Buy, take home, put in freezer — <–18°C

Questions

1 Compare the small kitchen method with the industrial method. List the differences in the cooking process between the two methods.

2 Why is a steam jacket used during the industrial cooking process?

3 What is the critical control point for this product? Give reasons for your answer.

Key points

● Large-scale recipes are developed from small kitchen recipes.

● The process for large-scale food production must be carefully controlled.

Large-scale canning, delivery and storage

5.1.2b, 5.1.7b, c, 5.1.8a, 5.1.9c, d, 5.2.1d, e, 5.2.1j, 5.2.2a–c, 5.2.3b

The Tarka Dhal produced by Patak's can be preserved by canning. The canned product does not have the same texture as the frozen product but may be more convenient to use.

Points in the process

The canned recipe uses both red lentils and yellow split peas because the yellow split peas can withstand the long sterilizing process without breaking down.

The canned product contains starch, which is a filling aid. The canned product has such a long, slow cooking process that the ingredients cannot be pre-cooked. The starch helps to hold up the other ingredients and stops them settling down during filling. The sterilizing process breaks down the starch again so that it does not appear when you eat the product.

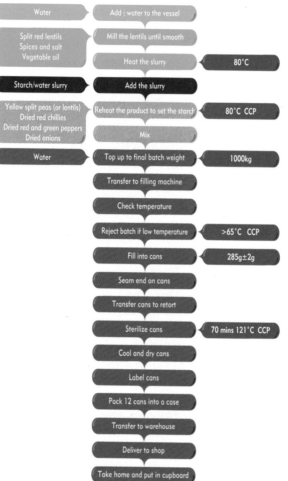

Chart used by Patak's in the production of canned Tarka Dhal – from ingredients to home cupboard

The label from a can of Tarka Dhal – note the modified maize starch in the ingredients

Delivering products

When the food product has been made and packed it is important to make sure that it is delivered safely and hygienically to the distribution point.

Food products can be delivered by air, sea, road and rail, all around the world, so there have to be strict guidelines to make sure the products arrive in good condition and are safe to eat.

Care during delivery

During delivery, food products should not be exposed to sun, wind or rain as this damages the packaging and product. Refrigerated vehicles often have special loading canopies to link them to the cold store to protect goods during delivery.

Frozen food needs careful monitoring to check on the temperature throughout delivery.

When the frozen goods are taken from the factory and stored in a cold store, the temperature of the cold store must be kept at –23°C or colder, and this temperature is monitored and logged. An alarm system warns if there is a breakdown. Temperature probes are used to probe into food to make sure it is the correct temperature. These probes must be accurate to 1°C and the results must be recorded, either automatically or manually.

Distribution vehicles are designed to control temperature so that the temperature of the frozen product is never higher than –18°C. Chilled products are delivered in temperature-controlled lorries, and temperatures must be monitored and recorded throughout the delivery process. These records are kept to use in evidence if there is an outbreak of food poisoning associated with the product.

Delays in delivery

The food industry has designed a computer program called Food MicroModel which can predict bacterial growth in food products. If a delivery is delayed, the company can phone the program hotline to find out if the product can still be delivered safely. Information on the product formulation, temperature and time are analysed by the program and the likelihood of bacterial growth is predicted. This is an example of computer **modelling.**

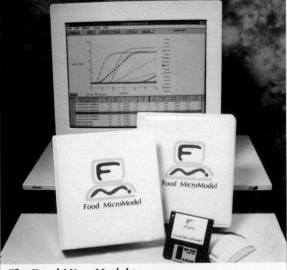

The Food MicroModel program

Storage

Products that are stored at ambient temperature (i.e. room temperature, 20°C to 25°C) include canned and dried food, bread, flour and sugar. These products are date coded to show their shelf life and do not need to be transported in chilled conditions. Care is needed to make sure that the packaging is not damaged so that the product is not infected with pests or micro-organisms. The packaging of these products needs to be designed to make sure that they stack easily and can be easily handled and carried.

Questions

1 What are the ingredients used for canned Tarka Dhal?

2 What is the cooking process for canned Tarka Dhal? What temperatures must be reached during cooking?

3 CCP means there is a critical control point in the process. This step must be carried out if the hazard is to be removed or reduced to a safe level. Describe the CCPs in this process and explain the likely hazards and how they can be reduced to a safe level.

4 What is the product's final batch weight?

5 What is the tolerance weight for filling the cans?

6 Explain how a frozen food product is delivered from factory to store and what temperature controls are needed during this process.

7 Why do food manufacturers keep such careful records of the temperatures of the food throughout delivery?

8 How can computers be used to predict the safety of a food product during delivery?

Key point

● Temperature control is measured throughout the process of delivering food so that the food is safe and quality maintained.

Packaging 1

Examples of various types of packaging materials

Reasons for food packaging

A food product needs packaging to:

- protect it from damage and so reduce food waste
- contain the food so that it is easy to carry
- keep bacteria and dirt away from food
- provide customers with information and attract them to buy the product
- help with transportation and storage
- increase the shelf life of the product.

Packaging must be easy to stack, store, distribute, use, open and reclose.

The rules for food packaging are described in the Materials and Articles in Contact with Food Regulations 1987. Packaging materials must be safe to use with food, and certain products must be packed to specific weights – for example, butter and sugar.

Package design takes many weeks and requires skilled operators. Many of the processes of making a package are controlled by computer.

Tamper evident packaging

Many packs of food are designed so that you can see if anyone has tried to open or tamper with them. You may get a tear strip around the top of plastic bottles or a plastic strip around pots of cream. If these are broken do not buy the product.

Examples of tamper evident packaging

Waste from packaging

Nearly 25% of household waste is made of packaging. Food producers are trying to reduce the amount of packaging used for their products.

Some of the types of packaging materials used for food

Types of packaging materials	Words to describe packaging
Paper	see-though, thick, thin, easy-to open, inexpensive, rigid, soft, recyclable, stackable, waterproof, solid
Board	colourful, protective, flexible, essential, luxury
Plastic	used in microwave, used in oven, porous, easy-to-print on, cheap, keeps food safe
Glass	strong, reusable, transparent
Metal such as foil and cans	lightweight

The packaging specification

In industry, the packaging specification provides detailed information of:

- the types of material used for the packaging, and the suppliers of the materials
- detailed labelled drawings of the packaging
- the process of making the packaging
- a copy of the label, which has been checked by the legal department of the company.

CAD and CAM

CAD (computer-aided design) and CAM (computer-aided manufacture) are systems used in designing and making packaging. CAD can be used to help design the layout, information and design of the food packaging.

The net for the packaging can be designed on computer and this information is transmitted to a card-cutting machine, which controls the cutting of the packaging shape for assembly. The net is the flattened shape which, when cut out and folded, can be made into a solid shape.

This is the process needed to make a folded carton.

- The structure of the carton is designed using CAD for the carton profile.
- This profile is multiplied many times and fitted together in such a way that many cartons can be cut from a large piece of paperboard with the minimum of waste.
- The paperboard is printed as a continuous sheet then varnished or waxed.
- This is then cut and creased – which requires great precision. The cartons are then separated from the paperboard sheet.
- If the carton includes glued side seams or bottoms, this is usually done on a special machine.

The carton is assembled by folding and stitching. This is done on the site where the packaging is needed, prior to packing and despatch of the finished product.

Computer controlled packaging manufacture

A system is needed to control the quality of the packaging as it is made:

Process	Controls	Check
Design the information for the packaging labels	Make sure the information meets the legal requirements	Ask local trading standards officer or research organization
Design the layout for the net	Make sure the net is measured exactly	Check by making a prototype
Make the packet	Cut and form accurately	Make sure it meets tolerance levels

Questions

1 What is the function of food packaging?

2 Why do manufacturers use tamper evident packaging?

3 How are CAD and CAM used for making packaging?

Key points

- Packaging is essential to make sure the food is kept safe and clean.
- Packaging provides information.

Packaging 2

 pp.83, 84, 85, 86

5.1.3g, 5.1.4e, 5.1.6f, 5.1.8c, d, f, g, 5.1.9c, 5.2.4e, 5.2.5f

The design and construction of packaging often takes longer than producing the food product, so package design must start early in food product development.

Designers must think about how the package protects the product, and work out an appropriate size, shape and construction. The label has to be attractive and provide useful information that also meets legal requirements. Environmental issues, such as avoiding too much waste, must also be considered.

'Consumer research is carried out with the designs to see if changes are needed and we then present the results to the client. Once the final idea is agreed we create the artwork, take photographs and put the text in place along with the legal labelling requirements and bar code. We have checked that the packaging can be constructed and once the client has approved everything the packaging is ready for production.'

Case study of package design

Design in Action (DIA) is a London-based design company. One of its specialist areas is food packaging. Jason Butler, the creative director for this area, explains how the team develops a piece of packaging design.

'The client gives us a verbal or written brief for the packaging and we work as a team to brainstorm ideas and develop a strategy for designing and making the packaging.

'We work out a time plan for the project, carry out market research, and create a key message (idea) for the package design. Checks are made at this stage to make sure the design can be manufactured. Then we meet the client to show them our ideas presented as mood boards with colours, shapes and images that we think represent the best solution for the product. At this stage the client will provide input and we agree a way forward. We prepare four to five designs for the packaging based on the key message, using a range of artwork and computer-generated letters and images. We work with the client in choosing one or two designs and then develop the prototype models to show how the finished packaging will look on all sides.

The finished package design

Getting help with design ideas

When designing your own packaging, a good way to begin is to make a collection of different types of food packaging. Do a product analysis to get information on packaging nets and how the packaging is put together. You may be able to use the packaging as the base of your own design.

Designing a food package

You can follow these steps to choose the food packaging for your product.

1   Decide how to process the food product for storage. Will it be chilled, frozen, stored at room temperature, canned, made into a long-life product, dried, bottled and stored in jars or vacuum packed in a pouch?
2   What packaging material is suitable for the type of processing you have chosen? For example, if the product is to be canned then you will need to choose metal cans.
3   The packaging may be made up of several parts. Internal packaging may hold the items, such as biscuits or cakes, and this may be wrapped then packed in a cardboard sleeve.
4   Do you want part of the packaging to be used as a container to reheat the food? If so, you will need to choose special materials. If the food is a ready-meal you will need to think about the shape of the container, so that you make it suitable to hold a meal.
5   Some foods, such as cook-chill meals, have a cardboard sleeve fitted round the inner tray. This sleeve provides information on cooking and storing the product.
6   Sketch and label your ideas. You can draw a net and design a food label that provides the correct information on your food product.

Using ICT

Computer programs can be used in many ways for packaging design in industry and at school. Some will help with the net design, or you can create the food label with text and graphics, and include photographs and drawings.

Packaging uses computer-aided design

Questions

1   Look at the case study opposite. Draw a flow chart to show the steps in the process of package design for a food product.
2   What are the advantages of using a computer to help with package design?

Key points

● Packaging is essential to protect the food product and provide information.

● Food packaging needs a detailed specification for production.

● Packaging design must be started as soon as a new food product is being developed.

● The design of the packaging matters almost as much as the food product – it can attract the customer to buy the product.

● Computers can be used to explore the use of packaging nets and create and manipulate images to use on packaging.

Food labelling

The Food Labelling Regulations describe the information that must be on a food label. These Regulations apply to almost all food for human consumption, with the exception of natural mineral waters and some other foods and food products.

By law a food label must contain the following information:

- the name of the product
- ingredients in descending order of weight
- the net weight of the product
- the name and address of the manufacturer, packer or seller
- the 'use by' or 'best before' date to identify the shelf life (durability indication)
- any special storage conditions or conditions of use.

This information must appear on the packaging, on a label attached to the packaging or on a label clearly visible through the packaging.

In certain cases the food label must also show:

- place of origin of the food
- instructions for use.

Nutritional information is voluntary unless a nutrition claim is made. The Regulations impose conditions for making claims such as reduced or low energy claims, protein claims, vitamin claims, mineral claims and other nutrition claims. The Regulations specify labelling requirements for nutritional information, whether or not a nutrition claim is made.

Consumer rights

People have a right to be sold quality goods and can return unsatisfactory products which do not meet quality standards. The Sale and Supply of Goods Act 1994 states that goods must be of satisfactory quality, fit for their purpose and as described. This Act helps consumers with their rights when they buy goods.

Quality standards

Throughout production, food is checked to make sure that it meets high standards of quality. Some food labels show a quality symbol.

BS EN ISO 9000

This is a series of Standards for Quality Systems which has British, European and International recognition. Food and drink product manufacturers are interested in meeting these standards in order to obtain certification which they shows they have reached a high standard of quality in their organization.

Date coding

Food labels carry date codes to show how old the product is. 'Use by' date codes are found on chilled foods, such as sandwiches and ready-meals, which should be stored in the refrigerator. The product is no longer at its best after the 'use by' date and should be thrown away. 'Best before' date codes appear on foods with a short to medium shelf life, such as bread, biscuits, crisps and sweets. 'Display until' date codes are used by the store to tell them when to remove the product from the shelves.

Examples of date codes on food labels

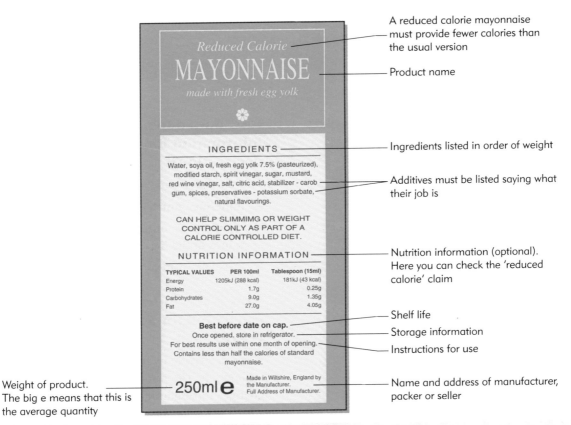

A reduced calorie mayonnaise must provide fewer calories than the usual version

Product name

Ingredients listed in order of weight

Additives must be listed saying what their job is

Nutrition information (optional). Here you can check the 'reduced calorie' claim

Shelf life

Storage information

Instructions for use

Name and address of manufacturer, packer or seller

Weight of product. The big e means that this is the average quantity

This label for mayonnaise shows how all the information has been put in place

Bar codes

A bar code is a symbol printed on packages which identifies the goods in a way that can be identified electronically or transmitted to a computer. Each bar code is unique and they are read by optical character recognition (OCR) equipment.

Bar codes help customers by providing a quicker checkout service, itemized till receipts, reduction in checkout errors and more efficient store operation. For industry, bar codes improve communication between manufacturer and retailer, improve stock control and allow for faster reordering.

This bar code is from a packet of crisps

Questions

1 What information do the Food Labelling Regulations 1999 require to be on a food label?

2 What is the importance of date codes on the label?

3 What is the difference between the different date codes?

4 Why is a bar code system useful for consumers and industry?

Key points

- The Food Labelling Regulations control what information is on a food label.

- Important information includes date coding to show the shelf life of the product.

Nutrition labels

The Food Labelling Regulations specify labelling requirements for nutritional information. Nutrition information is voluntary unless a nutrition claim is made.

Nutrition labelling may be given in two formats:

Group 1, also known as the 'Big 4' declaration

Nutrition information	
	Typical values per 100 g
Energy	kJ
	kcal
Protein	g
Carbohydrate	g
Fat	g

Group 2, also known as 'Big 4 + little 4' or '4 + 4'

Nutrition information	
	Typical values per 100 g
Energy	kJ
	kcal
Protein	g
Carbohydrate	g
of which sugars	g
Fat	g
of which saturates	g
Fibre	g
Sodium	g

The government recommends that Group 2 information is given on all foods on a voluntary basis as this gives consumers information on the key health-related nutrients.

Information must be declared per 100 grams or 100 ml of the food.

How does a manufacturer get the information for the nutrition declaration?

The company can:

- undertake nutritional analysis
- calculate the nutrients from known or average values of the ingredients
- calculate from established and accepted data.

How is the nutrition information calculated for a bag of ready-salted crisps?

Crisps are made by frying sliced potato in oil and adding salt. The nutritional value of potatoes changes throughout the year after harvesting, which will affect the nutritional profile of the crisps. To work out the nutritional value of ready-salted crisps, bags were taken at random from the production line from every shift during a week. This analysis was carried out every three months throughout a year. The analysis was carried out in a laboratory and the average value calculated. This is the information displayed on the label.

INGREDIENTS

Potatoes, Vegetable Oil, Salt.

NUTRITION INFORMATION

Typical Values	Per 100g	Approx per bag 25g
Energy	2380 kJ (570 kcal)	595 kJ (148 kcal)
Protein	5.8g	1.5g
Carbohydrate	52.5g	13.1g
Fat	37.5g	9.4g

The ingredients and nutrition information from a bag of ready-salted crisps

Nutrition claims on food labels

A nutrition claim means any statement, suggestion or implication in any labelling or advertising of a food that the food has particular nutritional properties. The Food Labelling Regulations 1999 impose conditions for making claims such as reduced or low energy claims, protein claims, vitamin claims, mineral claims and other nutrition claims.

You may want to make nutrition claims about a product. These are guidelines you can use:

- 'low fat' – total fat is less than 5 g per normal serving in which there is more than 100 g or 100 ml
- 'low sugar' – no more than 5 g in a normal serving of food in which there is more than 100 g or 100 ml
- 'reduced fat' – fat content at least 25% less than the regular product
- 'source of fibre' – either 3 g per 100 g or 100 ml, or at least 3 g in the reasonable expected daily intake of the food
- 'rich in fibre' – foods contain at least 6 g of fibre per 100 g or 100 ml.

Source: MAFF guidance notes on nutrition labelling and draft guidelines for the use of certain nutrition claims in food labelling and advertising

Note: On food labels and in food claims, NSP (dietary fibre) is called fibre. In this book, the term NSP is used in nutrition information and the term fibre for food labels.

Labelling for special dietary requirements

Special dietary information can be included on the food label to help people make food choices.

Labels show that food is suitable for vegetarians.

The product may be gluten free and this can be shown on the label.

Additive statements can be shown.

> No added colour, no added preservatives, no artificial flavours.

Some people have a particular food intolerance and need to know if a food product contains certain ingredients that they are unable to eat – such as peanuts or milk products. This information can be shown on the label.

> This product contains peanuts.

Calorie controlled diets

Some people are following a calorie controlled diet and need to choose products with a specific range of calories. This information can be shown on the label.

Keeping a check on labels

Trading standards officers are responsible for checking that products are properly labelled and show the correct weight and product information.

Questions

1. What is the value of providing nutritional information for food products?
2. Choose one nutrition claim. Describe the criteria that must be met by the product to meet that claim.
3. What information is available to meet special dietary requirements?

Key points

- Very detailed information is provided on nutrition labels.
- Nutrition claims must meet certain nutritional criteria.

Nutritional analysis

The label on a food product contains details of the nutritional content of the food. You can work out the nutritional content in a series of steps.

- List the exact amounts of food ingredients and water used in the recipe.

- Use *Food Tables* or a nutritional analysis computer program to get information.

- Choose the nutrients you want to analyse.

- Tip – use the same information as a food label.

- Big 4 label: energy kJ/kcal, protein, carbohydrate, fat.

- 4+4: energy kJ/kcal, protein, carbohydrate, of which sugars, fat, of which saturates, fibre, sodium.

- Work out the amount of nutrients in 100 grams of your food product.

- Work out the amount of nutrients in a portion of your food product.

- Use these results on the food label.

Using the computer

Nutritional analysis of food products involves complicated mathematics, so it is much easier to use a computer program for this task. Other benefits are listed below:

- using a computer speeds up the calculations for a quick comparison of results
- the computer should provide accurate results
- the computer can work out the nutritional value per 100 grams and per portion
- changes can be made quickly to model possibilities.

Modify the recipe

The screen shots show two recipes for apple crumble. The first apple crumble recipe has been modified in recipe 2 to increase the NSP (dietary fibre) content.

The white flour used in recipe 1 has been changed to wholemeal flour and some desiccated coconut has been added to the topping.

The computer program produces a label that shows the fibre content in 100 grams for each recipe.

Recipe 1 has 1.45 grams fibre per 100 g, and recipe 2 has 3.74 grams of fibre per 100 g. The modified recipe needs to be tested to see if it tastes all right before accepting these changes.

Recipe 1

Recipe 2

Food claims

The adapted version of apple crumble can now claim to provide a 'source of fibre' since it provides over the 3 grams of fibre per 100 g, which is the recommended limit for this nutrition claim.

When making your own food product it is useful to compare the nutritional value of your recipe with a ready-to-eat version.

Note: On food labels and in food claims, NSP (dietary fibre) is called fibre. In this book, the term NSP is used in nutrition information and the term fibre on food labels.

Key points

- Nutritional analysis can be carried out by manual calculation or using a computer.
- You can quickly compare recipes with ready-made products.

Questions

1 A ready-to-eat bread and butter pudding has the following nutritional analysis:

	Per 100 g
Energy	854 kJ
	204 kcal
Protein	5.2 g
Carbohydrate	21.6 g
of which sugar	13.4 g
Starch	8.1 g
Fat	10.8 g
of which saturates	5.9 g
Monosaturates	3.5 g
Polyunsaturates	0.5 g
Fibre	0.4 g
Sodium	0.3 g

Ingredients: water, bread, whipping cream, egg, sugar, raisins, skimmed milk powder, vegetable oil, butter, salt, mixed spice, colour annatto.

Here is the nutritional analysis of a home-made bread and butter pudding:

INGREDIENTS
Milk, Bread, Eggs, Sultanas, Butter, Sugar, Nutmeg.

NUTRITION INFORMATION
TYPICAL VALUES (COOKED AS PER INSTRUCTIONS)

	PER 100g	PER PORTION
ENERGY	706.18k J	1537.70k J
	167.68k cal	365.13k cal
PROTEIN	4.90g	10.68g
CARBOHYDRATE	22.45g	48.88g
of which SUGARS	13.87g	30.20g
FAT	7.17g	15.62g
of which SATURATES	4.08g	8.87g
FIBRE	0.41g	0.90g
SODIUM	0.18g	0.40g

If you compare the analysis of these two recipes you will see that the ready-made pudding has a higher energy value and more fat. If you look at the ingredients for the home-made recipe, you will see how the ingredients are different.

Compare the two products and show how the different ingredients affect the nutritional analysis.

2 What is the advantage of using a computer to calculate the nutritional analysis of a food product?

Nutritional modelling

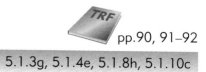

Using nutritional analysis to compare products is an example of modelling. Modelling is a way of translating ideas in your head into a form that other people can understand.

To carry out nutritional modelling:

- start with the exact recipe that you want to investigate and find its nutritional value
- decide what changes you want to make to the nutritional profile; you may want to…
  - lower the fat
  - increase the fibre
  - lower the sugar
  - increase the minerals or vitamins
  - make the product suitable for someone on a weight-reducing diet
- take the recipe and change one ingredient
- compare this result against the original recipe and try another idea if necessary.

Modifying a recipe

This example investigates how to lower the fat in some cheese straws.

1 The original recipe is analysed.

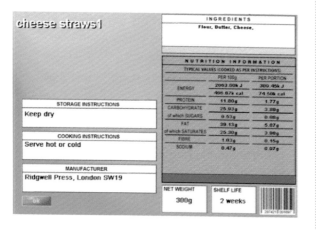

2 Now the amount of cheese in the original recipe is reduced to 75 grams and replaced with a strong flavoured cheese.

Cheese straws2

INGREDIENTS
Butter, Flour, Cheese.

NUTRITION INFORMATION
TYPICAL VALUES (COOKED AS PER INSTRUCTIONS)

	PER 100g	PER PORTION
ENERGY	2047.67k J	307.15k J
	493.00k cal	73.95k cal
PROTEIN	11.40g	1.71g
CARBOHYDRATE	25.93g	3.89g
of which SUGARS	0.53g	0.08g
FAT	38.90g	5.83g
of which SATURATES	25.10g	3.77g
FIBRE	1.03g	0.15g
SODIUM	0.46g	0.07g

STORAGE INSTRUCTIONS
Keep cool.

COOKING INSTRUCTIONS
Serve hot or cold

MANUFACTURER
Ridgwell Press

NET WEIGHT	SHELF LIFE
300g	2 weeks

3 Then the cheese is changed to a lower fat cheese but the original amount kept the same.

Cheese straws3

INGREDIENTS
Flour, Butter, Cheese.

NUTRITION INFORMATION
TYPICAL VALUES (COOKED AS PER INSTRUCTIONS)

	PER 100g	PER PORTION
ENERGY	1857.33k J	278.60k J
	446.33k cal	66.95k cal
PROTEIN	13.80g	2.07g
CARBOHYDRATE	25.90g	3.88g
of which SUGARS	0.50g	0.07g
FAT	32.67g	4.90g
of which SATURATES	21.20g	3.18g
FIBRE	1.03g	0.15g
SODIUM	0.47g	0.07g

STORAGE INSTRUCTIONS
Keep cool

COOKING INSTRUCTIONS
Serve hot or cold

MANUFACTURER
Ridgwell Press London

NET WEIGHT	SHELF LIFE
300g	2 weeks

4 The next idea is to try lowering the fat in the recipe. This will obviously change the fat content but it may also affect the recipe. Only 50 grams of butter is used and water is added to mix the dough.

Cheese straws4

INGREDIENTS
Cheese, Flour, Butter, Water.

NUTRITION INFORMATION
TYPICAL VALUES (COOKED AS PER INSTRUCTIONS)

	PER 100g	PER PORTION
ENERGY	1730.83k J	233.88k J
	415.37k cal	56.08k cal
PROTEIN	13.02g	1.76g
CARBOHYDRATE	28.81g	3.89g
of which SUGARS	0.59g	0.08g
FAT	28.35g	3.83g
of which SATURATES	18.11g	2.45g
FIBRE	1.15g	0.15g
SODIUM	0.39g	0.05g

STORAGE INSTRUCTIONS
Keep cool

COOKING INSTRUCTIONS
Serve hot or cold

MANUFACTURER
Ridgwell Press

NET WEIGHT	SHELF LIFE
270g	2 weeks

5 Now the nutritional profiles are compared to see the effect of the changes.

6 Compare results. Compare the same quantity each time. In this case the nutritional value per 100 grams is a sensible comparison.

7 The final step is to test the recipes and see how the changes affect the sensory qualities of the product. The reduced-fat cheese straws may not taste very nice!

The results: fat per 100 g

Original	Recipe 2	Recipe 3	Recipe 4
39 g	39 g	32 g	28 g

You can see that the most effective way to reduce the fat was to lower the amount of butter in the recipe.

Cheese straws

Ingredients
100 g Cheddar cheese
100 g plain flour
pinch salt, pepper and cayenne pepper
100 g butter or margarine

Method

1 Set the oven at 180°C (gas mark 4).

2 Grate the cheese finely.

3 Sieve together the flour, salt, pepper and cayenne pepper into a bowl.

4 Cut the butter into small pieces, add to the bowl and rub in with your fingers until the mixture resembles breadcrumbs.

5 Add the grated cheese and knead the mixture until it forms a stiff dough.

6 Flour the work surface and roll the dough out until it is a square about 20 cm by 20 cm.

7 Cut into 16 equally sized strips.

8 Place the strips on a baking tray and cook for 10–12 minutes until golden brown and crisp. Cool on a wire rack and pack in an airtight box.

Questions

1 Suggest other ways the cheese straws recipe could be modified to make nutritional changes.

2 How can you work out the nutritional value of each cheese straw?

Key points

- A computer can show nutritional modelling for a food product.
- Using a computer, results are accurate and quick.

Questions

Spaghetti Bolognese

This is a list of ingredients for spaghetti Bolognese made from a meat sauce with spaghetti.

Ingredients

200 g minced beef
100 g chopped onion
1 clove garlic
50 g tomato paste
salt
pepper
100 g spaghetti

You have been asked to present ideas to package this product as a ready-meal.

1　Suggest different ways that the product could be packaged. Give reasons for each of your answers.

2　Choose one of the methods of packaging and draw a labelled diagram to describe what the packaging is made from and how it is constructed.

3　Suggest ways that the spaghetti Bolognese could be processed to make it into a ready-meal. For each idea, give the shelf life, storage and reheating instructions.

4　For the food label, list the ingredients in order of weight.

5　Carry out a nutritional analysis of the product.

6　Draw up a detailed food label to show what other information you will include.

Chicken burgers

Ingredients

50 g fresh wholemeal breadcrumbs
2 chicken breasts (about 280 g meat) skinned and minced or finely chopped
50 g mushrooms very finely chopped
salt and pepper
wholemeal flour for rolling out
a little oil for frying

Method

● Put the breadcrumbs, chicken, mushrooms, salt and pepper in a mixing bowl and mix thoroughly.

● Sprinkle flour on the work surface and shape the mixture into a roll. Cut into four equal sized pieces and shape into burgers.

● Heat a very little oil in a frying pan and cook each burger on each side for 6–7 minutes. Alternatively, brush with a little oil and cook under the grill.

● Serve hot.

7　Draw up a flow chart to show how to make these chicken burgers.

8　Show what safety and quality checks are needed for each stage.

9　Draw up a HACCP chart for the preparation of this product.

10　What equipment is needed to make this product?

11　How could the manufacturer reduce the cost of this product?

12　Give two suggestions to show how the product could be prepared for sale and the type of packaging that could be used.

13　Suggest two ways that the product can be prepared for eating.

INDUSTRIAL CASE STUDIES

New Covent Garden Soup Company

The launch of a new soup: the design process

In 1997, the New Covent Garden Soup Company began the development process for a new Malay-style soup that could be sold for about £1.55 a carton.

The new product development department (NPD) developed the recipe and worked out how to scale up the recipe from the kitchen stage, through to the factory stage. NPD is responsible for finding new ingredients that might be necessary for the development of the soup, and for working out an initial idea of costs. Technical staff work out specifications for ingredients and quality control. The public relations department makes sure that the soup is promoted in the media – for example, coverage in magazines. The commercial department works out the final cost and negotiates all the ingredients' costs. The production department is responsible for making the product. All members of the team are important in the development process.

The research and tasting resulted in a Malay-style soup, which is a hot soup with a variety of vegetables in it. It contains no preservatives, colourings or other additives.

For the development of this product, the company drew up a project plan showing the stages of development:

Some definitions

Analytical testing involves the nutritional analysis of the product. The results of this analysis are used on the packaging.

Formulation approval means that the soup has been tasted and it has been agreed that it is ready for launch. Various factors are taken into consideration to get to this stage, including tasting by members of relevant departments and consumer research.

Stages	Months							
Acceptance of brief	Oct							
Research		Nov						
Product development		Nov						
Ingredient sourcing		Nov						
Kitchen development		Nov	Dec					
Review meeting			Dec					
Factory development			Dec					
Analytical testing				Jan				
Review meeting				Jan				
Packaging development				Jan				
Packaging design					Feb			
Formulation approval						March		
Artwork						March		
Proofing							April	
Launch								May

This is called a Gantt chart and shows the time scale for developing, producing and launching a new product.

Specifications are needed for all raw materials. Costing and nutritional information are also needed. The recipe is developed and tested several times, and people taste and offer their comments. A tasting chart asks for comments on appearance, texture and flavour. Here are some of the comments:

'I like the little bits of chilli – it's very hot!'

'Could we add some more mushrooms?'

Once the exact factory recipe has been approved, the nutritional information can be worked out to use on the label. An ingredients list is given to the marketing department so that this can be added to the packaging design. A detailed quality plan with checks is written. This will include the following points:

- the weight of the cartons must be checked regularly as they are filled
- each batch of soup needs to be checked for viscosity, particulates (the pieces of ingredients visible in the soup) and colour
- when the soup is chilled it must be below 4°C, which is tested with a temperature probe.

A detailed product description is written.

- Consistency – describes the soup and any particulates in it.
- Particulates – what kinds of vegetables or herbs are floating in the soup?
- Mouthfeel and texture – what does it look like, how does it feel when it is eaten, has it got particulates, is it brothy, is it creamy?
- Colour – to be compared with a colour chart and to have a description of the colour of the product. For example, 'it looks like curry', 'the colour of terracotta'.
- The microbiological standard for the soup is calculated and the soup given eighteen days shelf life.

Everybody involved with the product development then signs to show that all the stages have been completed. The product is now ready for launch.

The finished product

Questions

1 Describe the process of designing and launching a new soup.

2 What is a Gantt chart and why is it useful?

3 Describe the sensory properties for the following products using the headings Consistency, Mouthfeel and texture, Colour, Flavour, Particulates:

a tomato ketchup

b minestrone soup

c cheese sauce

d sweet and sour sauce.

Key points

- The process for designing a new soup is very organized and mapped on a Gantt chart.
- Detailed product descriptions are needed.

Muffin making

This case study looks at how carrot and orange muffins are made on a large scale. They are sold ready-wrapped and will keep fresh for about ten days. The work is adapted from *Food in Focus: Cakes and Muffins* by Hazel King, published by Heinemann Educational.

The ingredients:

- finely milled cake flour
- sugar
- eggs
- oil
- grated carrot and orange peel.

The process

1 The dry ingredients are weighed then blended with the eggs and oil to make a batter.

2 The batter is poured down a depositing machine. The muffin cases are placed under the nozzle, which is controlled by a foot pedal. This releases the right amount of mixture into the case.

3 The tops of the muffins are sprinkled with large sugar granules called sugar nibs.

4 The muffins on the baking trays are placed in a rotary reel oven. The shelves rotate in a circle. The muffins bake at 180°C for 35 minutes.

5 The baking trays are taken out and the muffins cooled and placed on a conveyor belt.

6 When cold, they are sealed with plastic in a flow-wrapping machine, the label is stuck on the packet and they are packed ready for delivery.

7   Lorries take the muffins to a distribution centre and they are delivered to supermarkets and other outlets.

Sweet muffins

This is a basic recipe for sweet muffins. You can add a variety of flavours such as chocolate chips to this recipe.

Ingredients

150 g white self-raising flour
$\frac{1}{2}$ teaspoon baking powder
75 g granulated sugar
1 medium egg
3 tablespoons vegetable oil (45 ml)
150 ml semi-skimmed milk

Method

1   Set the oven at 200°C (gas mark 6).

2   Brush the muffin tin with a little oil to stop the muffins from sticking.

3   Sieve the flour and baking powder into a bowl and add the sugar.

4   In a measuring jug, beat the egg and mix in the oil and milk. Stir thoroughly into the flour mixture.

5   Spoon the mixture into the muffin tin. Fill each hole until the mixture is near the top.

6   Bake on the top shelf for 20–25 minutes until the tops are golden and the mixture springs back when touched. You can test by inserting a skewer, which should come out clean from the muffin mixture. Leave the muffins to cool slightly before removing them from the tin. Cool on a wire rack.

Questions

1   Suggest three sweet and three savoury recipes for muffins which you think would be popular if they were sold in a school canteen. Give reasons for your choices.

2   Draw a chart to show the steps in large-scale muffin making and describe the controls you think are needed for each step.

3   Draw up a chart for small-scale muffin making. Complete a chart like the one below to show the equipment used and the quality checks that are needed.

Key points

- Muffins can be made in factories on a large scale.
- Temperature and time controls are important.

Process	Equipment needed	Quality checks
1 Set the oven at 200°C (gas mark 6)		Check the time taken for the oven to heat up.
2		
3		

Making cannelloni

Making a cook-chill ready-meal

The cannelloni in this case study is a chilled ready-meal made from fresh egg pasta with beef and tomato filling and a creamy sauce, topped with Parmesan cheese. This is an example of batch production.

The specification that the factory uses to make this dish is 20 pages long. The specification provides information on suppliers, details of the recipe (including step-by-step quality checks) and details of how the products are packed. A tolerance of 2 mm in length is given on the cannelloni tubes and 2 grams tolerance in weight. The two sauces – béchamel and tomato – must be heated to, and held at, 90°C for 3 minutes and the cannelloni filling must be cooked to 70°C minimum. The Parmesan cheese must be positively cleared microbiologically to make sure it is safe to eat. Each day, the product is tasted and three samples are tested for bacteria. Three times a week, samples are taken from each product line to test for food poisoning organisms and the product is tested each month to make sure the meat content is the same.

The process

Making the beef and tomato filling

The beef comes from approved and inspected suppliers and chunks of meat are minced in the factory. The minced beef is fried in huge pans until it browns.

Mincing the beef

Vegetables used in the filling include onions, celery and carrots. The crates of vegetables are checked for quality. Rejected vegetables go back to the supplier.

The celery is put into an automatic washing drum and soaked in chlorine solution to kill bacteria. Then it goes into a mechanical dicer.

The onions, celery, carrots and vegetable oil are put into one of the 200-gallon steam-heated vats containing mechanical mixers. The vegetables are cooked until they are softened. The chefs test the vegetables by tasting to see if they are soft enough. Pre-weighed oregano, black pepper, salt and basil are added to the vegetables. These products are packed in blue plastic bags so that any scraps of plastic can be spotted if they fall into the mixture.

The chef pours in tomato purée, tomato juice, cooked tomatoes and the cooked minced beef. This mixture is poured into trays, taken to a steam-heated oven and cooked for one and a half hours at 100°C. The mixture is tested with a temperature probe to make sure it reaches the 70°C minimum limit. It is then chilled to below 5°C.

Making the pasta

In the dry goods area the semolina is passed over a metal detector then it is mixed with water, salt and pasteurized egg to make the pasta. The dough is kneaded in a machine then sheeted (rolled) and cut and blanched in boiling water to soften it. Next the cannelloni is filled with the meat mixture so it looks like a long sausage. It is then chopped into portions.

Packing up the pasta

The foil pack is filled with a layer of tomato sauce, cannelloni, béchamel sauce and then Parmesan cheese is sprinkled on by hand. The lid is fitted, the pack weighed, scanned by a metal detector and the outer packaging added.

Production line workers place the cannelloni rolls into foil trays

Batches go into the blast chiller at a temperature of –10°C for an hour. Electronic temperature probes are plunged into samples which are then thrown away. This provides a safety check. The cannelloni is stored in the despatch room at 2°C. It has a sell-by date of six days and must stay at a temperature below 5°C.

The quality assurance manager tests a sample from the first batch of cannelloni

Samples of the cannelloni are tested for bacteria in the microbiological laboratory

Distribution

Cook-chill meals must be transported in refrigerated lorries, which are cooled with liquid nitrogen to a temperature of 1°C or below. The products in the lorries are checked on arrival and if any product is higher than 5°C the food technologists must consider the safety of the product and decide if it is to be thrown away. The cannelloni is taken into the cold store of the supermarket and then taken to the chill cabinets by the shelf stackers. These cabinets are checked up to nine times a day to make sure that they run at –2°C to 2°C. The cabinets are linked to automatic alarms which ring if the temperature rises too high.

Questions

1 Describe the temperature checks that are made during the production of cannelloni.

2 Draw a list to show the stages in the process for making the cannelloni.

3 What control checks are needed for each stage?

4 How are the following components made:

  a the filling

  b the pasta?

5 How is the final product made up, chilled and stored?

6 How is the product transported to the store?

Key points

● Hygiene and safety are important throughout the production process.

● Temperature controls are essential throughout the process.

Noon Products Ltd

Designing and making vegetable jalfrezi and masala dal

Noon Products Ltd is a company that specializes in making chilled and frozen Indian ready-meals. The products are developed from traditional recipes using authentic ingredients and cooking methods that bring out the flavour in the product. No artificial additives or preservatives are used.

The large recipes are scaled-up versions of kitchen recipes and the making process for the large-scale version follows traditional methods.

The factory

There are low-risk (blue) and high-risk (red) areas in the factory. The food is cooked in the low-risk area and stored in the high-risk area.

People work in an air-conditioned room at 9–12°C and the air is filtered so that no smells go outside the factory.

Making the product

This product is made from mixed vegetables cooked in a north-Indian-style sauce. The product is served with chick pea lentils and kidney beans. This is how the product is made.

- The ingredients arrive from the store room and are checked against the specification.
- The product is cooked in two stages – the vegetable jalfrezi and the dal.
- Large blenders are used for grinding garlic for the purée.
- The jalfrezi and the dal are cooked in large Bratt pans, in the stages specified in the recipe. Chefs stir the food with a big paddle. First the spices are fried in oil with onions to bring out the flavour, then the other ingredients are added and simmered until soft.

- The components of the product are chilled on trays in a blast chiller to less than 5°C for 4 hours. They are then removed for filling.

Ingredients for Noon brand vegetable jalfrezi

Ingredients	Batch amount	Ingredients	Batch amount
Baby corn	17 kg	Green peppers	8 kg
Beans	17 kg	Jeera powder	1.2 kg
Cauliflower	17 kg	Kasturi methi	0.2 kg
Chilli powder	0.2 kg	Oil	12 kg
Chopped tomatoes	44 kg	Onion puree	13 kg
		Red peppers	8 kg
Cumin seeds	0.6 kg	Salt	1.2 kg
Dhainya powder	1.2 kg	Sliced onions	35 kg
Fresh coriander	2.6 kg	Tomato puree	14 kg
Garam masala	0.2 kg	Turmeric	0.3 kg
Garlic	2.4 kg	Vinegar	3.3 kg
Ginger	3.3 kg	Water	27 kg
Green chillies	0.6kg		

Checking the spices for the vegetable jalfrezi

116

This is a recipe that you could scale down and cook for yourself. Notice the range of traditional spices and herbs used.

Filling and packaging

Packing is carried out in the high-risk area. The inner dish used for the packaging can be cooked in an oven or microwaved. Packaging must be easy to hold and carry and be safe to use with food.

The jalfrezi and dal are carefully measured into the dish to an exact weight. Each dish is put through a sealing machine. The top film is sealed on by heat and excess film cut off. All packs are checked through a metal detector and weight checker. The outer carton is placed over the dish and the product can be either stored in a chiller or frozen.

HACCP

Every stage in the process has to be analyzed so that the HACCP chart can be drawn up. This chart ensures that all risks and hazards have been identified, assessed and controlled to make a safe product. Below is a section from part of the chart for the filling operations:

Hazard	Critical limits	Monitoring procedures	Frequency	Corrective action
Filling operations Microbial growth due to rise in product temperature	Packing room temperature must be between 8–12°C. Product should maintain a temperature below 5°C during filling operation.	Check using a probe and record on temperature checklist. Only one tray of vegetables must be in the filling station.	Every 2 hours.	Inform the engineering section. If air temperature continues to rise, remove product to chiller.
Freezing operation Inadequate freezing	Product should achieve a minimum of –18°C before cartoning. Product can either be frozen in blast freezer set at –24°C or turbo freezer set at –40 to –42°C. Label with title and pack date.	Probe meal from trolley. Record temperature on daily production sheet.	One meal from every trolley used. Every half hour.	Put product back in freezer until temperature is achieved.

The packaging for the finished product

Questions

1 What are the main ingredients in the vegetable jalfrezi and masala dal?

2 What is the purpose of HACCP and how is it used to produce this product?

3 Describe how the product is packed, sealed and stored.

Key points

● HACCP is an essential part of any product planning.

● Every stage of production needs detailed analysis.

117

Cake making

Three of Cherry Willink's cakes

Hamburger and chips cake

Roller skate cake

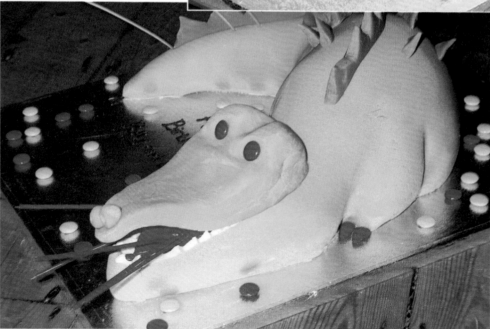

Green dragon cake

Cake making

Cherry Willink runs a cake design business making special 'one-off' cakes for birthdays, weddings and parties. This is an example of job production (also known as 'one-off', 'jobbing' or 'craft' production).

Do people know what cake design they want?
'Some people, especially children, know what they want and I get sent drawings or models to show how the cake should be made. Most people need help, so we talk or they come to visit and get ideas. I ask them who the cake is for and if they have got special interests or hobbies which help with the cake design.'

How do you work out design ideas?
'I sometimes draw ideas and write down special points. I designed the roller skate cake for a ten-year-old girl who loves skating. The cake is modelled on the roller skates she was getting for her birthday.'

How do you work out the costs?
'I price the cake according to the amount of work involved in the construction and icing design. At this stage I give the customer an estimate of the cost and this can change if the cake takes longer.'

How are the cakes made?
'The cakes are either sponge or fruit cakes and I bake them in round or square shapes. I then use butter icing, moulded icing and glacé icing and maybe sweets in the design.

'Ben's hamburger and chips cake is made from two round cakes which are covered with different coloured icing to look like a bun with a burger and cheese. I've used red glacé icing for the ketchup and made the chips from yellow moulded icing.

'The green dragon is made by cutting up sections of cake and decorating it with green moulded icing. I've used red and green candles down the spine and in the mouth of the dragon.

'Finally the customers come and collect the cakes ready for the celebration.'

What do you enjoy about making these cakes?
'People are usually very pleased when they see their cake and I like being creative and making up the different designs.'

What problems do you face with 'one-off' products such as cakes?
'It is difficult to earn very much money. People will pay about £50 for a cake but it can take ten hours to make it so the cost includes my work and the ingredients. It can take a long time to research and discuss the cake design and this needs adding to the cost.

'Some people don't realize how long a cake takes to make. You can't just order it for the next day – it can take one to three weeks to make.

'The design can be a problem. Some cakes don't work! For example, the open mouth on the dragon cake was very difficult to shape without it falling down. Also customers don't know exactly what they are going to get, so you may run the risk of them not liking it.

'The market in speciality cakes has changed. Supermarkets are making speciality cakes that are cheaper as they can be mass produced.'

Questions

1 Use this case study to list the steps in the process of making a 'one-off' speciality cake.

2 Suggest how you would make one of the cakes shown here.

3 Comment on the problems that face a designer who is making 'one-off' products such as cakes. Could this situation be changed? Give reasons for your answer.

Key points

- One-off food products are complicated to design and make.

- It is quite difficult to make a profit from such design work.

Large-scale cake decorating

How are cakes filled?

Chocolate eclairs and other cakes and pastries often have fillings. To carry this out on a large scale, manufacturers use machinery that injects the fillings into the baked products. The injectors can work vertically for a cake filling, or horizontally to fill croissants, buns and chocolate eclairs.

How are cakes decorated?

Special machinery is designed to decorate cakes in several layers. The cakes can be filled in layers with cream and jam and various types of icing.

The cakes travel along a conveyor belt building up layers of filling and decoration.

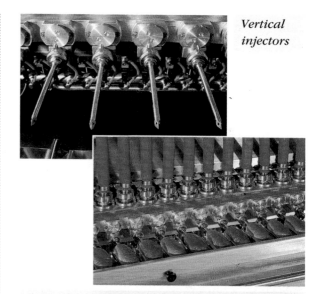

Vertical injectors

Vertical injectors are used to fill chocolate eclairs

These cakes are mass produced on a conveyor belt system

The cakes are sliced automatically.

The first cream layer is deposited and then levelled to make it evenly distributed.

The second layer is deposited and levelled.

The final layer of cream or icing is squeezed on and any decorations such as nuts are sprinkled on the top.

This machinery can decorate 1800 cakes an hour.

Questions

1 How would you carry out the following processes if machinery was not available for the task? Describe the equipment you would need for each task:

   a slicing sponge cakes in half

   b spreading filling on to cakes

   c piping icing on to the top of the cake

   d decorating with chopped nuts.

2 Describe three advantages of using machinery for the production of an iced cake.

Key point

● Computer-controlled machinery can produce high quality, accurate results for food products.

Biscuit making

Large-scale equipment for cutting and shaping

Just a few of the many different biscuits available

Basic biscuits are made from flour and water, and this recipe can be changed by adding fat, sugar and flavourings such as jam, chocolate and coconut. When you make biscuits on a small scale the recipe determines how you cut them out or shape them and how long, and at what temperature, they are baked. If you make biscuits on a small scale you can:

- roll and cut them out with shaped cutters
- measure spoonfuls of soft dough
- pipe them into shapes
- roll out balls of dough by hand.

For mass production, machinery takes over these processes. Here are three different methods of preparing biscuit dough for the oven.

- The dough is rolled out by a sheeter and then fed through two rollers. The first roller marks a pattern on the biscuit and the second rotary cutter cuts out the biscuits, which pass onto a conveyor belt and into the oven.

A rotary cutter

- A wire cutter cuts the dough into shapes. The dough is extruded down pipes, and the wires cut through the dough and the cut pieces drop onto the conveyor belt and into the oven.

- Biscuits that are made from a soft batter can be squeezed into portions using a dosing unit.

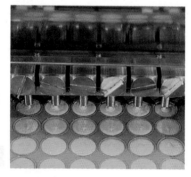

A dosing unit

Other methods of shaping biscuits include a rotary moulder and a rout press.

A rotary moulder

122

Cooking in the oven

Biscuits can be baked by direct or indirect heat. The gas flame in direct ovens is in the same chamber as the biscuits. Indirect ovens have fans which circulate the hot air. These ovens have different heat zones so products may be baked first at a high temperature and then cooked at a reduced heat to complete the baking process.

A type of travelling or tunnel oven is used to cook biscuits and cookies.

The dough is fed automatically from the bowl into the rotary moulder and the biscuits are cut into shape. The biscuits may be glazed with egg in the egg washing unit, then coated in sugar by the sugar sprinkler.

They pass to the large tunnel oven for baking. This oven is heated by oil, electricity or gas and is divided into zones so that the biscuits can be cooked at different temperatures at various stages of baking.

These ovens allow the biscuit to bake evenly so that they do not burn easily. They also have a large capacity so that many biscuits can be baked at the same time. Inspection doors are found around the oven so that the operators can check on the cooking process. After baking, the biscuits are cooled and then packed.

Adding extras

Some biscuits are filled with creams. The base biscuit passes under a tube that deposits the cream, then the biscuit passes on down the conveyor and the top biscuit is added. A little pressure is needed to squeeze the parts together.

Coating with chocolate

Biscuits can be fully or part coated with chocolate. There are two main types of chocolate coverage – enrobing and moulding. For enrobing, the biscuits are taken on a wire mesh into the enrobing machine and they pass through a curtain of chocolate. Excess chocolate flows through the mesh into a bath below. As the biscuits pass over this bath the bottom of the biscuits is coated with chocolate. For moulding, the biscuit is placed into a mould that has been coated with chocolate. More chocolate is deposited on top to give a fully covered product. The mould is cooled and the biscuit released from the mould.

Biscuits are enrobed in chocolate

Thank you to DATA for permission to adapt this text from *Food Technology in Practice*

Questions

1 If you had to make biscuits by hand, describe the steps in the process. Explain what could affect each stage in the process that would change the quality of the finished product.

2 How can machinery that is controlled by computer produce a biscuit that looks and tastes the same every time?

3 How are biscuits made into different shapes?

4 How is a chocolate biscuit made?

Key points

- A variety of equipment has been designed for large-scale cutting and shaping of biscuits.

- Large ovens control the cooking time and temperature to produce a perfect result.

Questions

Making sliced bread

This diagram shows how sliced bread is made in a factory. The basic ingredients are flour, salt, improver (which speeds up the breadmaking process), yeast and water.

A computer system controls the process to make sure that the loaves of bread have the same texture, taste and weight every time. These bakeries often work twenty-four hours a day, seven days a week.

1 How are the ingredients measured and mixed?

2 Explain how the dough is divided and placed in tins.

3 What is the purpose of proving the dough?

4 Why does a baked loaf pass through a metal detector?

5 Why are the loaves of bread cooled before they are sliced?

6 How are conveyor belts used for the breadmaking process?

7 What control checks do you think are needed during the breadmaking process?

1 Delivery and storage
Flour arrives at the bakeries in tankers and is stored in silos before it is sifted.

2 Weighing and mixing
Flour and water are automatically measured. All the ingredients are mixed to a dough in a high-speed machine.

3 Cutting and shaping
The dough is divided into loaves, shaped and dropped into tins. Most sliced loaves have flat tops. To achieve this a lid is placed on top of the tin.

4 Proving and baking
The loaves move by conveyor belt to a proving area where they increase in size. The tins pass through a hot oven where they are baked.

5 Cooling down, inspection, slicing and packing
The loaves are cooled and pass through a metal detector. Sharp blades slice the loaf according to thickness. Thick sliced bread is often used for toast and thinner slices are used for sandwiches. The bread is bagged, labelled and loaded onto vans for delivery to supermarkets and shops.

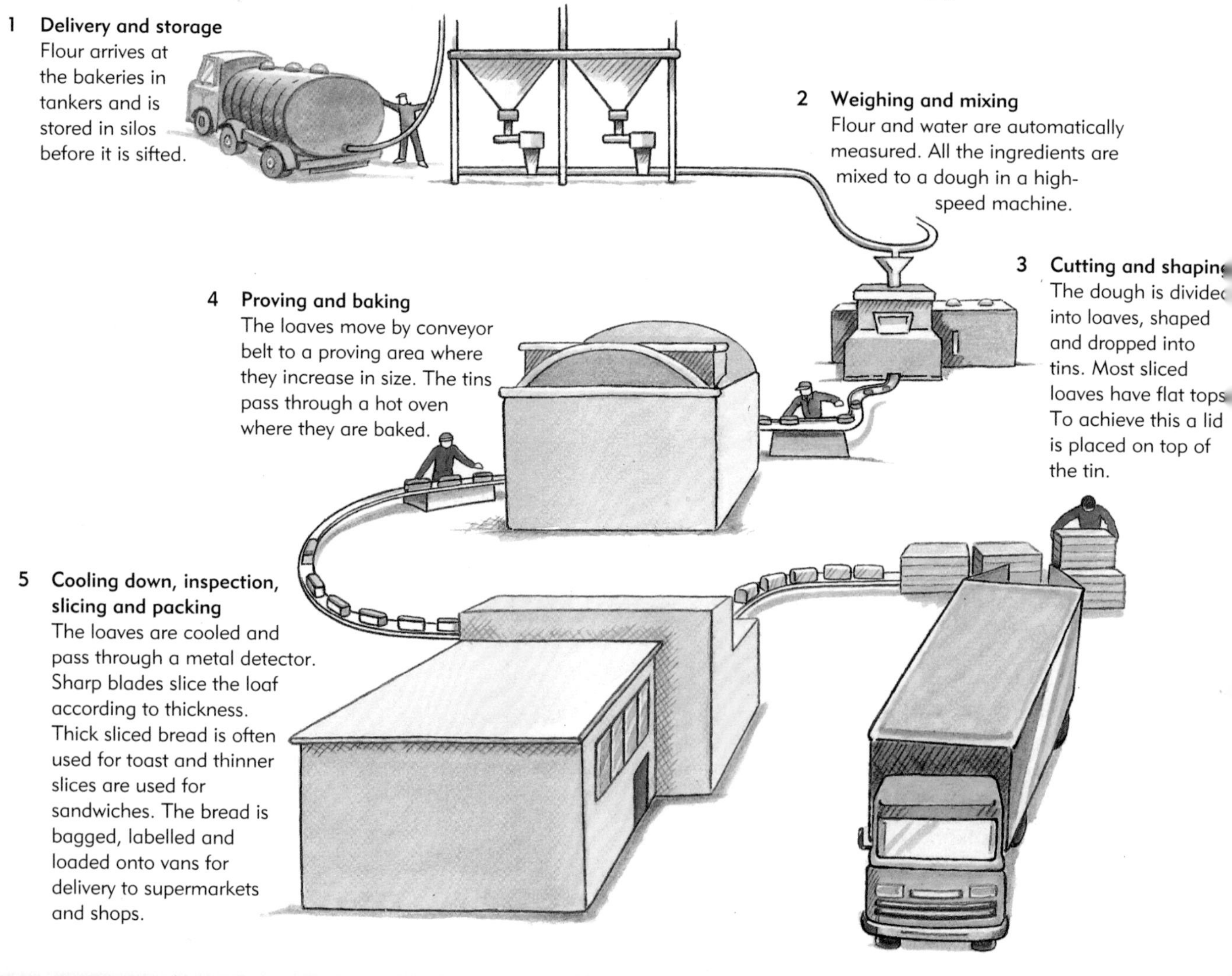

FOOD TECHNOLOGY SKILLS

Product analysis and concept screening

p.93

5.1.2a–d, 5.1.3a–d, f, 5.2.3a, d, 5.2.4a

Product analysis

Product analysis can help:

● to get design ideas

● to find out how products are made

● to work out specifications by weighing and measuring other products and looking for ways to improve them.

When food producers want to design a new food product they often buy a selection of similar food products and take them apart. If a supermarket chain wants to design a new range of pasta dishes, they might buy pasta dishes from other supermarkets and even restaurants. A design team then takes the product apart and looks at the different pasta shapes used and the sauces and other components. They could measure the weight of the ingredients used and use the results to come up with their own ideas.

How do you analyse food products?

Product analysis can be carried out in stages.

1 Look at the product and its packaging. What is it made from, how is it made and who would buy it?

2 Look more carefully. Draw, measure, weigh, label and describe what you see.

3 Take the product apart and weigh the components.

4 Describe how the product tastes. Remember to cook it first, if necessary.

5 Use the packaging to find out the ingredients used, the nutritional value and the weight.

All this information can be used to produce a specification.

When you have carried out this detailed analysis, you can work out the function of the ingredients in the product and compare one product with another. The product analysis may also help you to understand how the product is made.

The drawings show the different type of information you can get when you analyse two types of Cornish pasty. You can find out details of size, shape, weight of pastry and filling, and details of the filling ingredients that have been used.

Mini Cornish pasty

74 g:
24 g filling,
50 g pastry

Potato, cheese and onion pasty

153 g:
30 g filling,
123 g pastry

Packaging analysis

You can get lots of information by making a packaging collection and then undoing the sections. Label your findings to help with your design ideas.

Concept screening

Concept screening is a technique used in industry to sort through all the design ideas and help come up with a few ideas to test and trial. It helps to focus design thinking and only develop products that are needed. Here is the design brief for the example of concept screening shown below.

Design brief

To develop a range of savoury, vegetarian products for teenagers, which can be cooked in the microwave.

This diagram shows you how and why products were rejected at each stage.

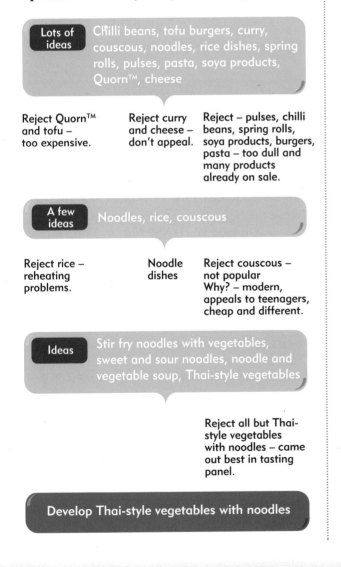

Lots of ideas
Chilli beans, tofu burgers, curry, couscous, noodles, rice dishes, spring rolls, pulses, pasta, soya products, Quorn™, cheese

Reject Quorn™ and tofu – too expensive.

Reject curry and cheese – don't appeal.

Reject – pulses, chilli beans, spring rolls, soya products, burgers, pasta – too dull and many products already on sale.

A few ideas
Noodles, rice, couscous

Reject rice – reheating problems.

Noodle dishes

Reject couscous – not popular
Why? – modern, appeals to teenagers, cheap and different.

Ideas
Stir fry noodles with vegetables, sweet and sour noodles, noodle and vegetable soup, Thai-style vegetables

Reject all but Thai-style vegetables with noodles – came out best in tasting panel.

Develop Thai-style vegetables with noodles

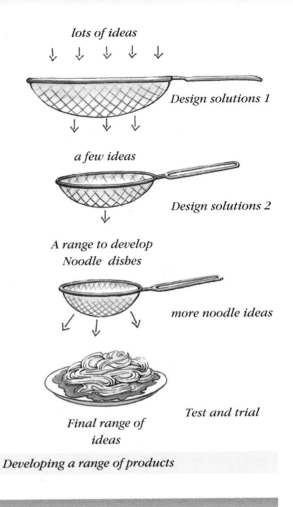

lots of ideas

Design solutions 1

a few ideas

Design solutions 2

A range to develop Noodle dishes

more noodle ideas

Final range of ideas

Test and trial

Developing a range of products

Questions

1 Make a list of the information you can obtain by carrying out product analysis on:

   a a food product

   b packaging.

2 What is meant by the term concept screening and how is it used by the food industry?

Key points

● Product analysis helps to find out more about a product.

● Concept screening is a way of sorting through a lot of design ideas to find a few to test and trial.

Modifying a food product

5.1.3c, f, 5.1.4d, 5.1.10c

There are many types of modification that can be carried out on a food product. You can modify:

- the ingredients – to change the taste and colour of the product
- the nutritional status – to increase or decrease certain nutrients to meet the design brief
- the cooking method or time – to improve the product
- the shape of the product – to get better results
- the finish of the product – to improve the look.

In the food industry, products are modified for many reasons, such as to:

- change the amount of additives used
- reduce the cost of the product by using cheaper ingredients
- make the product suitable for different dietary needs
- include new ingredients
- change the proportions of certain ingredients
- make a product that is more efficient for the machinery to be used.

Food labels sometimes show that a product has been changed:

New improved recipe

Modifying the ingredients and the cooking method

This **star profile** shows the results of making and tasting egg and cheese noodles. You can see how the recipe needs to be changed to meet the design profile. When trialling a product you need to try out these changes and test the product again.

Egg and cheese noodles

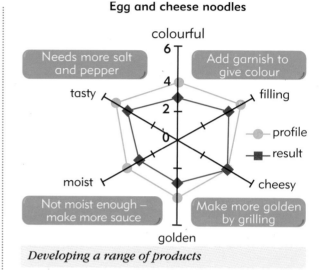

Developing a range of products

Modify the nutritional status of the product

If you want to change the nutritional status of a recipe, you must know the exact amount of the ingredients to carry out the nutritional analysis. Summer pudding recipe 1 has been modified to change the NSP (dietary fibre) content.

Note: On food labels NSP (dietary fibre) is referred to as fibre, in line with government guidelines.

Summer pudding recipe 1

serves 4
650 g raspberries
75 g sugar
8 large slices white bread (36 g a slice) = 288 g

Summer pudding recipe 2 (modified to increase fibre)

serves 4
650 g raspberries
75 g sugar
8 large slices wholemeal bread
    (36 g a slice) = 288 g
60 g coconut, desiccated

Summer pudding recipes modified to try to increase NSP (dietary fibre)

Per 100 g	Energy		Protein	CHO	Sugar	Fat	Saturates	Fibre	Sodium
	kJ	kcal	g	g	g	g	g	g	mg
Recipe 1	479.2	112	3.3	24.7	8.7	0.6	0.2	2.0	149.8
Recipe 2	583.1	137	3.6	21.7	8.5	4.2	3.2	3.8	151

CHO = carbohydrate

Evaluation of modification

By changing the bread to wholemeal and adding coconut to the mixture, the NSP (dietary fibre) content has increased. However, the fat has increased too! Tests must now be carried out to see if the product tastes all right as the coconut could make the product dry.

Changing the shape

Traditionally, scones are cut into small, round shapes. To make production more efficient, two alternative shapes have been chosen for trialling. A hexagonal cutter will be used and also the dough is to be patted and shaped without cutting. The results can be taste-tested to see if this production method is successful.

Hexagonal scone cutters reduce waste

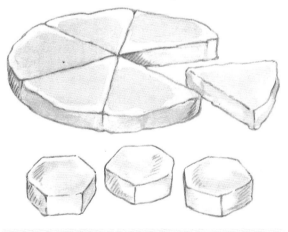

Alternative scone shapes

Questions

1 Give three reasons why a food company would want to modify a food product.

2 Do you think consumers prefer hexagonal or roughly shaped scones? Give reasons for your answer.

Key points

● There are a number of reasons why food products are modified.

● Products are always taste-tested after any modification.

From recipe to outcome

 pp.94, 95, 96, 97, 98

5.1.5a, 5.1.7c, 5.1.8h, 5.1.10a

When designing food products, you often use and adapt recipes to meet the needs of the design brief. The example shown is developed for a brief that asks for ideas for desserts that are higher in NSP (dietary fibre) than traditional dishes.

Summer pudding

The recipe

Summer pudding is traditionally made from layers of white bread with a filling of soft summer fruits such as strawberries, raspberries and blackcurrants. The summer pudding recipe 1 (page 128) will be adapted for the design brief.

Changing the ingredients

The ingredients will be changed by replacing the white bread with wholemeal bread and adding coconut to the filling.

Changing the shape

Traditionally the recipe is made in a pudding bowl but this shape is difficult to divide into sections, so this recipe is made by layering the bread and fruit in an oblong tin.

Changing the method

The method needs to be changed to take account of the changes in ingredients and shape. Only one method of cooking the fruit will be chosen instead of a choice between microwave cooking and boiling.

The modified summer pudding recipe shown on this page will be used for the final product.

High fibre summer pudding Serves 4

Equipment
Sieve, chopping board, sharp knife, bowl with cling film, tablespoon, oblong dish, plate and weight

Ingredients
650g soft summer fruit such as strawberries, raspberries and blackberries
75g sugar to sweeten
10 large slices wholemeal bread
60g desiccated coconut

Method
1. Place the fruit in a sieve and wash gently in running water to avoid damaging the fruit
2. Place the fruit in a microwavable bowl and cover with plastic film. Cook until the fruit is soft. Stir occasionally.
3. Stir the sugar into the fruit and leave the fruit to cool.
4. Remove the crusts from the slices of bread and cut into thick strips about 3–4 cm wide. Press the strips of bread into the base and sides of the dish.
5. Spoon in the fruit and cover the top with more strips of bread. Place a plate on top of the summer pudding and put something heavy on top of the plate, such as a bage of sugar. Leave in a cool place for several hours.
6. Remove the plate. Using a knife, loosen the sides of the summer pudding. Place a large plate on top of the dish and turn the pudding upside down onto the plate.

Planning a control system

The food product needs charts to show how a control system is used in the making process. You can complete a chart such as the one shown below.

Planning and flow charts

In the food industry, charts are set up to show safety and quality checks as well as HACCP for food products. These charts are essential to try to ensure a safe, quality product is made every time and the charts are used as evidence that the company has shown due diligence when planning the production of the product.

Some simple HACCP charts and safety and quality checks for the summer pudding are shown opposite. The Teacher's Resource File has proformas for these charts.

Tips for using ICT

The charts shown opposite are similar to the ones used in industry and can be quickly copied and adapted for each purpose using a word processing package on a computer to cut and paste the repeating sections in the charts.

Control	How?	Why?
1 Weighing and measuring ingredients.	Use scales, jug and teaspoons.	To achieve accurate quantities of ingredients so products are all the same.

Key points

- Recipes need adapting for design work.
- You need a control system and planning and flow charts.

Costing a food product

pp.99–100

5.1.2b, c, 5.1.3g, 5.1.4e, 5.1.8h

Cost is important when you are designing products for sale. In the food industry, there is no point making a product that is too expensive for people to buy or setting a price that makes no profit. If you are designing a **marketable product,** then you need to calculate the cost of the ingredients and work out the likely selling price.

Costing a recipe

List the quantities of the ingredients used in your recipe, find out how much they each cost and calculate the total cost. You may need to modify your recipe if you cannot make it cheaply enough to sell – in other words, if your product is not marketable.

How to cost a food product

Quorn™ stir fry (serves 4)	cost
142 g Quorn™	1.60
4 tablespoons olive oil	0.04
100 g bean sprouts	0.16
$\frac{1}{4}$ large pepper	0.12
60 g broccoli	0.16
1 clove garlic	0.02
Total	2.10
Total per portion	0.53

Help from computers

A computer program such as Microsoft Excel can be used to set up a spreadsheet for costing recipes. Keep a record of the cost of ingredients on a spreadsheet and then you have a ready-to-use system for costing recipes.

Some supermarkets have a home shopping service. Tesco offers 20,000 products online and they produce a CD-ROM. This provides up-to-date information on the cost of products, which you can use for your work. You can obtain this information from their website at http://www.tesco.co.uk. Other supermarket chains operate Internet based home delivery services and you can use their websites to check the latest food prices and new lines – this should also help you research new food trends.

Large-scale food costs

The selling price of a food product must include a variety of costs. These include:

- ingredients
- packaging
- distribution costs
- advertising
- labour
- factory costs
- marketing
- the retailers' cost and profit.

The pie chart shows the breakdown of one food company's costs. You can use this as a rough guide to work out the selling price of your food product if you know the total cost of the ingredients.

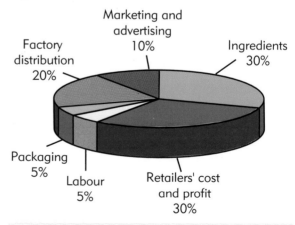

A breakdown of the selling price of a food product

A screen from the Tesco website

Working out the selling price of your food product

Food companies can buy their ingredients much cheaper than you can from a supermarket, so how do you work out the estimated selling price of your product? This formula was created by a food designer.

1 Calculate the cost of the recipe, based on supermarket ingredients.

2 Take off 30% from that cost – this will give you the cheaper price that you might pay if you bought in bulk.

3 Multiply this lower cost by three to give you the selling price.

Note: The pie chart and the formula offer slightly different ways of calculating selling prices.

This is because people in the food industry use different methods for calculating the final cost. The selling price of food products can vary enormously and often depends on how much profit the company wants to make.

Question

1 Work out the possible selling price for the Quorn™ stir fry costed in the chart on the opposite page.

Key points

- The cost of ingredients is an important factor in product design.

- Industry must add the costs of overheads, marketing and retailers' profits to work out the selling price.

Food tasting 1

 pp.101, 102–03, 104, 105, 106–07

5.1.3e, 5.1.4a, 5.1.7d, 5.1.10c, 5.1.11d, 5.2.1b, 5.2.4e

Sensory analysis

Tasting food for product development is known as sensory analysis. Sensory analysis is used throughout food product development to make judgements about the quality of food.

Everyone's taste is slightly different, so when food is tasted professionally, the tasting panel should agree on the terminology used to describe food.

Sensory descriptors

When we taste food, we are judging several factors:

- appearance and colour
- taste and flavour
- mouthfeel/texture, consistency
- smell or odour.

The words used to describe these factors are known as **sensory descriptors.** Each factor uses different sensory descriptors:

- appearance and colour – attractive, healthy, greasy, creamy, golden, orange, bright, dull
- taste and flavour – fruity, sweet, bitter, sour, salty, sharp, spicy, tangy
- mouthfeel/texture, consistency – hard, soft, rubbery, crispy, lumpy, dry, smooth
- smell or odour – fragrant, burnt, herby, garlicy, fishy.

Colour

We expect food to be a certain colour and may reject it if the colour is not familiar. We might reject raw apple that had gone brown, or green custard, because these are not colours that we would expect. Food manufacturers add colours to some food products, such as canned peas, to make them more attractive.

You can decorate the food with garnish to add colour to the dish. Savoury garnishes include twists of lemon or cucumber, slices of tomato, chopped parsley, and fried onion rings. Fresh, sliced fruit can be used to garnish sweet food.

Tasting tips

- Carry out tastings hygienically and if possible use a tasting booth.
- For tastings use tasting equipment such as spoons, paper towel, paper cups, plates and labels.
- Make sure the tasting is fair – food samples should be served at the same temperature in similar containers and labelled with a random code.
- Hot food should be served hot, and not left to keep warm and become dried up. Cold food should be kept chilled until it is ready to serve.
- Get several people to taste your food – this gives a range of views.
- There are different types of test, such as ranking or rating tests to see which product people like best.
- Use tasting descriptors to help describe your product.
- Use a star profile to see if the product meets the specification.
- Record the tasting results on paper or on a computer spreadsheet.
- Present the results attractively.

Food tasting chart (tick a box for each section)

	Like very much	Like moderately	Neither like nor dislike	Dislike	Dislike a lot
Overall opinion of food					
Appearance					
Taste					
Smell					
Texture					

Above is an example of a tasting chart that can be used to test food products.

This tasting chart can be filled in to give descriptions of a product.

Product:	
Appearance and colour:	Taste and flavour:
Mouthfeel/texture, consistency:	Smell or odour:

Tasting in the food industry

Tasting is a very important activity when designing new products and evaluating existing products. Here are some reasons why the food industry tastes products:

● new product development – to taste and develop a range of new products

● improving products – finding ways to develop existing products

● to reduce cost – to try to change the price of the product without affecting the taste

● a change in the making process – if the process changes the taste might change

● changing ingredients – if the company has a new supplier, taste tests are needed

● to compare competition – supermarkets compare own-label products with other **brands**

● to find out what consumers want – asking consumer taste panels what they like to eat

● to select the best ingredients – tasting to see which ingredient is the most suitable.

A food industry team carrying out sensory analysis

Questions

1 Make a list of descriptors for the following food products. Consider appearance, colour, taste and flavour, smell and texture. Food products: **a** pancakes with lemon **b** raita **c** sausage roll.

2 Explain why the food industry tastes food products – give five different reasons in your answer.

Key points

● Sensory analysis is carried out through different tests using tasting panels.

● Sensory analysis is used to develop new food products and to test the quality of existing products.

Food tasting 2

pp.101, 102–03, 104, 105, 106–07

5.1.4a, 5.1.10c, 5.1.11d, e, 5.2.1b, 5.2.3b, d

Different tests are used in sensory analysis to obtain different kinds of information.

Ranking test

This test sorts foods into an order. For example, the taster could be asked to place five yogurts in the order he or she likes the best. The taster could also be asked to rank the yogurts in order of sweetness.

Ranking test	Name _____	
Please taste the samples and put them in the order you like best.		
sample code	order	comments
○		
□		
△		
■		

A ranking test

Rating test

In this test the foods are given a score on a scale of say one to five. The scale could be shown graphically and the taster has to mark the point on the line that seems appropriate. When tasting cheese the graph could be:

extremely .... extremely
strong   mild

This is an example of a five-point rating scale:
1 = like a lot
2 = like a little
3 = neither like nor dislike
4 = dislike a little
5 = dislike a lot

Rating test				
	○	□	△	■
1 like a lot				
2 like a little				
3 neither like nor dislike				
4 dislike a little				
5 dislike a lot				

A rating test

You can use pictures to help with the rating:

Rating Score	1 😊	2 🙂	3 😐	4 🙁	5 ☹️
sample △					
sample □					
sample ○					

A rating test using pictures

Star profile

A star profile can show the sensory descriptors for the food. People on the tasting panel can rate each sensory descriptor to give the product a tasting profile. The results can be compared to see what people think about the product.

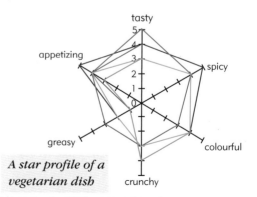

A star profile of a vegetarian dish

	Taster 1	Taster 2	Taster 3	Taster 4	Taster 5
tasty	3	4	4	3	5
spicy	4	5	5	4	4
colourful	4	4	4	4	3
crunchy	3	4	3	4	3
greasy	2	1	2	1	3
appetising	4	4	5	3	4

This star profile and spreadsheet chart shows how you can present the results of five people's views after tasting a product such as vegetable casserole.

Triangle tests

Triangle tests are used to see if people can tell the difference between food products. For example, can you tell the difference between one brand of crisp and another? These tests are used by food companies when they want to develop a 'me too' product – one that may be similar to another on the market.

Triangle test

Name Bill Jones

Two of the samples are the same.
One is different. Tick the odd one out.

Samples	Tick the odd one out
259	
372	✓
864	

British standards

There are several British standards which provide guidelines for the methods of sensory analysis of foods. These are found under British Standards 5929, 1992 and include: Part 1 – general methodology; Part 2 – paired comparison test; Part 3 – triangle test; Part 6 – ranking test; part 7 – investigating intensity of taste; Part 8 – duo-trio tests.

Top takeaway pizzas

In a food tasting, 29 families tried out a range of takeaway pizzas. There were two adults and two teenagers in each family. They ordered two thin-cut, cheese and tomato pizzas and two thick-cut, pepperoni pizzas made with pepperoni, cheese and tomato. Each person filled in a detailed questionnaire stating which pizzas they preferred and why.

Results

Some people liked more cheese on their pizzas and others liked more tomato. The pizzas that looked the best scored the highest marks. They like generous toppings, and pizzas that were moist rather than crispy. Less popular were pizzas that were too dry or too salty with thin toppings, a hard crust and too much cheese or grease.

The teenagers preferred cheesy pizzas and the adults liked stronger flavours. The pizzas were rated for taste, texture and overall preference, and comments were made on the amount of cheese, tomato and flavour along with other comments.

Source: *Which? Report*, December 1998

Questions

1 The pizzas survey used a questionnaire to get information. From the information above, write a questionnaire that would get the information required in the survey.

2 Why were the pizzas removed from the delivery boxes before the tasting took place?

3 Draw a star profile to show what kind of pizza people like the best.

Key points

● A range of methods is used to analyse tasting information.

● Several people should be involved in tastings to give a range of views.

Food photography

Photographs provide clear records for food work. You can photograph food at different stages when you are designing and making food products.

- For research, photograph a range of products to help give you design ideas.
- Keep photographic records of choices of ingredients to show how you make design choices for food products.
- Keep photographic records of experimental work and food trials during product design.
- Photograph finished results.
- Photograph tasting procedures.

Photographs can be used to support coursework.

- If you want to evaluate your work, mount the photograph of the finished result and present your comments around the photograph.
- A photograph of finished work can be used as part of the food label.
- You can use a series of photographs to show the production line for your product.

Using a digital camera

The cost of producing printed results in colour or black and white from a digital camera is much cheaper than the cost of producing photographs from traditional cameras. For schoolwork the digital camera is a valuable piece of equipment since many aspects of food design work can be recorded, and pictures can easily be pasted into product reports, packaging labels, sent via e-mail and used for presentations.

Use a digital camera to:

- provide pictures for product development
- record research
- produce product reports
- show a food system
- provide photographs for food labels
- record evidence of experiments
- show the finished product
- produce presentations of food technology work
- send as e-mail for research.

Ridgwells Rock cakes

6 in the pack   Best before 1st July 1998

Store in a cool, dry place

Nutritional information	nutrition per 100 g	Per rock cake (50g)
Energy kJ	1637	825
Energy kcal	389	196
Protein g	5	2.6
Carbohydrate g	55	28
Fat g	18	9
Fibre g	1.6	0.8
Sodium mg	322	162

Ingredients
SR white flour, soft margarine, sultanas, caster sugar, egg

0112 0059

A photograph of finished work can be used as part of the food label

Choose from a range of coloured pasta shapes

Scanned images of ingredient choices for a pasta dish

What paper to choose?

The quality of the image from the camera depends upon the type of paper you choose for printing using an inkjet printer. You can buy special photographic quality paper for printing images that look like photographs.

Using a video camera

A video camera can be used to record the process of research, experimental work, making a product and the final design outcome. These images can be incorporated into computer presentations as shown on screen.

Using a scanner

A scanner attached to a computer can scan in photographs which can be adapted for use with written work. You can also scan in images of actual food. Protect the scanner with a piece of clear acetate film to prevent food pieces entering it. You can scan sections of baked food such as scones, bread and cakes to show the effect of using different raising agents. You can also scan in a selection of food ingredients such as different coloured pasta to show how you would make food choices for recipes.

Using photographs in industry

A photograph of a food product can be used to keep a record of how the product should look. This photograph is part of the specification and is kept on file. It also helps to maintain the quality. A factory needs to design systems for checking the production and quality control as well as hazard analysis. This can be done using a series of photographs of the factory production line with details showing how the checks are made at each stage. 'Quick' photographs are used to show the professional photographers how the picture should be taken if it is used on a food label.

Questions

1. Suggest three ways that food photography can help when designing and making food products.

2. How can a scanner be used for food design work?

3. How is photography used by the food industry to record food work?

Key points

- Photographs of food products are important for food design to help maintain quality and standards.
- Industry uses food photography in many stages of food production.

Using ICT 1

A computer can be used in many ways to improve and speed up food work and aid Design and Technology activities and should be used where appropriate throughout your GCSE course.

What are the advantages of using ICT for Food Technology work?

- Using a computer speeds up the time it takes to carry out many tasks.
- Computers give greater accuracy when calculating information such as nutritional analysis and costs.
- Better quality work can be produced with well presented information.
- Graphs and pie charts can be produced quickly.
- Ideas can be modelled – such as nutritional comparisons and packaging designs.
- Food photographs can be taken using a digital camera and imported quickly into coursework to keep a record of work in progress and finished results.
- Work can be stored, copied and changed quickly to allow for adaptations in ideas.
- Tasting results can be analysed quickly and results presented graphically.
- Star profiles, which are useful for displaying design criteria and tasting results, can be drawn much more quickly using a computer.
- Clip art and flow chart images speed up the drawing process.
- Food labels can be created using DTP, photographs, text and imported images.
- A scanner can be used to import images into coursework.
- The final presentation will look smart and professional.

Teenagers' image board

This image board has been designed using clip art

The table opposite shows types of programs and equipment which can be used in different ways.

Questions

1 Explain how you would use the following types of program for food technology work: a database; a spreadsheet; a graphics program; computer aided design; control programs.

2 How could you carry out computer modelling for food technology work?

Key points

- There are many ways to use ICT to develop work for food technology.

Type of program	How can it be used?
Word processing	Word processing can be used for writing letters, creating questionnaires, and writing up coursework. Text can be produced in appropriate styles and sizes for presentation. Cutting and pasting text can save time when designing planning charts.
Database For example: **a** nutritional database **b** recipe database **c** information search	**a** Nutritional database – used to analyse recipes and modify them to make them healthier, or for working out a daily diet, or for menu creation. **b** Recipe database – for storing recipes and identifying ingredients. **c** Information search – databases available on CD-ROM, encyclopaedias, up-to-date information on food issues for research.
Spreadsheet graphics from spreadsheets	Spreadsheets are used for calculations such as the cost of a recipe, how to increase the size of a recipe to serve larger numbers of people and costing a product for sale. You can quickly display the information on a spreadsheet in the form of graphs, pie charts and radar charts, and present results in graphical form. Star diagrams are particularly useful for design work and tasting. This improves the presentation and accuracy of your work.
Graphics program	This can be used to produce drawings, **logos** and package designs and for experimental work in colour for labels. Images can be scanned in using a desktop scanner and adapted on screen. You can use a paint or draw program to produce original artwork including line, texture and coloured images.
Desktop publishing (DTP)	Coursework can be presented very smartly using a desktop package. Text and pictures can be created on the screen and the page layout designed. Blocks of text can be moulded and different sizes and styles of fonts chosen. Graphics can be added to suit requirements. Questionnaires can be designed and graphics and written work combined.
Computer-aided design (CAD)	Create and manipulate a range of 2D/3D images producing accurate drawings. This can be used for packaging design and to trial packaging nets.
Clip art	Clip art can be used for image boards that show design ideas. Clip art can also be used on labels.
Control programs	Special programs can monitor temperature changes in food as it cooks and record the results and display them on a screen or printout.
Modelling	For Food Technology, a simple spreadsheet can be used to model different recipes to compare the costs and the nutritional value. This saves time compared to calculating results by hand.
Using a scanner	Results of experiments can be scanned in and compared – for example, different recipes for scones or bread. Images can be scanned in for coursework and for label design.
Using a digital camera	The camera can record the results of practical work, take photographs for research and provide images for labelling.

Using ICT 2

Using ICT in the food industry

Here are some of the ways that information technology is used in the food industry:

- market research surveys and results
- process management in the factory
- modelling bacterial growth to determine food safety
- costing food products
- temperature control and monitoring changes
- distribution management – keeping records of where food products are being sent and stored
- stock control – shops monitor the amount of goods in stock and order more when needed
- nutritional analysis of food products
- bar codes – these help with stock control and ordering
- artwork designs and packaging designs can be transmitted around the world using a phone line.

Using the Internet

The Internet can provide a wide range of up-to-date information on the food industry and help with coursework research. The research for this book included searching the Internet for information. The latest food safety laws and guidelines can be found, along with information on food manufacturers and their products.

Tips on using the Internet for information

1 You can type in the website address to get specific information on a company or product.

2 If you don't know the website address, search for sites that might be close to what you want to find. For example, you could type in CAD+CAM and get lots of information from around the world.

3 You can guess at the website for a company by typing in their name, and sometimes adding '.co.uk'. Even if you don't find exactly what you want, you will be searching through information and discovering things about your research. You will find websites that have just been started and maybe some that are out of date.

4 When you have found a good website, make sure you jot down the website information. You can save it under 'Favourites' on the toolbar.

5 You can find the most popular websites visited in your topic area.

6 Collect website addresses by looking in magazines, catalogues and on packaging – the number of websites is increasing rapidly.

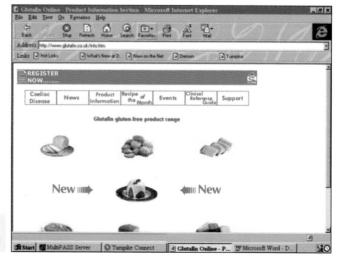

The Glutafin website (see table for address)

142

Note: These website addresses were checked before publication but site addresses do change.

1	Asda	http://www.asda.co.uk
2	Birdseye	http://www.birdseye.com
3	British Egg	http://www.britegg.co.uk
4	British Nutrition Foundation (BNF)	http://www.nutrition.org.uk
5	Boots	http://www.boots.co.uk
6	Campbell Soup Company	http://www.campbellsoups.com
7	DATA food website	http://www.foodtech.org.uk
8	Design and Technology Association (DATA)	http://www.data.org.uk
9	Food Allergy Network	http://www.foodallergy.org/
10	Food Forum	http://www.foodforum.org.uk
11	Food Standards Agency	http://www.foodstandards.gov.uk
12	Fresh fruit and vegetables	http://www.ffvib.co.uk
13	Glutafin – information on coeliac disease and gluten-free products	http://www.glutafin.co.uk/info.htm
14	Iceland	http://www.iceland.co.uk
15	Kellogg's	http://www.kelloggs.co.uk
16	Kraft Foods	http://www.kraftfoods.com
17	Leatherhead Food Research Association	http://www.lfra.co.uk
18	MAFF: National Food Survey	http://www.maff.gov.uk
19	Marks and Spencer	http://www.marks-and-spencer.co.uk
20	McDonald's Corporation	http://www.mcdonalds.com
21	Meat and Livestock Commission	http://www.britishmeat.org.uk
22	National Dairy Council	http://www.milk.co.uk
23	Nestlé	http://www.nestle.com
24	Public Health Laboratories	http://www.phls.co.uk
25	QCA	http://www.qca.org.uk
26	Ridgwell Press	http://www.ridgwellpress.co.uk
27	Sainsbury's	http://www.sainsburys.co.uk
28	Seafish	http://www.seafish.co.uk
29	St Ivel	http://www.st-ivel.co.uk
30	Tesco	http://www.tesco.co.uk
31	The Federation of Bakers	http://www.bakersfederation.org.uk
32	Unigate Dairies	http://www.unigate-dairies.co.uk
33	Unilever	http://www.unilever.co
34	United Biscuits	http://www.unitedbiscuits.co.uk
35	Vegetarian society	http://www.veg.org
36	Waitrose	http://www.waitrose.co.uk

The design process for a food product

5.1.1a, d, 5.1.2a, b, d, e, f, 5.1.3a–d, g, 5.1.4a, c, e, 5.1.5a, 5.1.11b, e

The table opposite shows the stages you might use when designing and making a food product to meet the needs of a design brief that has come from a project task for *OCR Design and Technology: Food Technology GCSE Internal Assessment (Coursework)*.

Marketable products

A marketable product is one that appeals to people and will sell when it reaches the shops. To succeed, products must be marketable.

Planning and presenting coursework

Coursework needs careful planning. There is a lot of research, testing and trialling to be carried out. Find different ways to present this information so that you can cut down on the amount of written work.

For example, for tasting comments you could take a photograph or make a drawing of the recipe, place it on paper and add your comments around the edges.

Tasting notes

Good colour and texture

Good combination of vegetables

Nice and crunchy

Tasting comments can be presented as a labelled drawing or photograph

Full course and short course

If you are doing the short course your internal assessment (coursework) should be no more than 20 hours work. If you are doing the full course it should be no more than 40 hours work. For both the full course and short course you should make sure all six objectives are covered (see pages 146–156). However, for the short course for most of the assessment objectives you are asked to produce less than for the full course. Where each assessment objective is outlined on the following pages (146–156) it will state which are full course only requirements and outline any differences between the full and short course.

How to do it	
Internal assessment objective 1 Identify a need or opportunity leading to a design brief.	Provide relevant information about the situation and the target group using a range of techniques or methods – e.g. questionnaires, graphs, photographs, drawings and written information. Show you have analysed this information before writing a clear and precise design brief for a marketable product.
Internal assessment objective 2 Research into the design brief and come up with a design specification.	Explain the purpose, form and function of the product. Evaluate existing products against the needs of your target group. Collect relevant data that will help you when developing ideas. Create a design specification using the results of research and analysis and include details of how your product could be made in batches.
Internal assessment objective 3 Generate design proposals.	A range of design proposals is needed to check against the specification which then may need to be modified. Then identify a chosen design proposal to take forward for product development. Present your proposals using a range of graphic techniques and ICT.
Internal assessment objective 4 Product development.	Investigations, trials and tests lead to choices of materials, production methods and pre-manufactured standard components. A prototype is developed and tested to make sure that it meets the original design brief. Consider the implications for quantity manufacture and develop a control system for manufacture of your product. Make any necessary modifications to your design and give details of it, including a final product specification. Present your final solution using a range of graphic techniques and ICT.
Internal assessment objective 5 Product planning and realization.	Create a flow chart using the standard symbols. Include manufactured items, materials, equipment, tools and processes. Include quality and safety checks. Work skilfully, efficiently and safely. Present the final packaging idea.
Internal assessment objective 6 Evaluating and testing.	Check that the final product (food and packaging) meets the original design brief and product specification. Taste and test using the target group, and consider whether improvements are needed to the product (food and packaging) and the control system.

Adapted from *OCR Design and Technology: Food Technology GCSE Coursework*

In order to come up with a design brief from a task, you need to provide a detailed description of the situation using a variety of methods – for example, text, drawings, graphs and possibly photographs. This should lead to the identification of a need or opportunity. A detailed description of the situation and the user can lead to a clear design brief for a marketable product.

From task to design brief

These two pages refer to coursework for OCR Food Technology, Internal assessment objective 1: Identify a need or opportunity leading to a design brief (4 marks).

In order to come up with a design brief from a task, you need to think carefully about the task and come up with needs or opportunities that will result in the design brief. You should then provide a detailed description of the situation, using a variety of methods – for example: text, drawings and graphs. You need a detailed description of the situation and the user, and a clear design brief for a marketable product.

This is an example of the development of Internal assessment objective 1 for the following task:

Task

As concerns about the health of the nation increase, supermarket chains have responded by selling healthier food products. However, research shows that some people continue to eat food products that do not always meet the current dietary recommendations. The marketing department of a supermarket has asked you to address this problem.

For this task, Internal assessment objective 1 can be carried out by:

- Researching information on healthy eating – reports, current dietary recommendations, effects of the diet on health etc.

- Designing a questionnaire to find out about people's eating habits and to identify a gap in the market for a healthy food product.

Questionnaires should be given to a minimum of six and a maximum of 10 people.

- Analysing the results of research to identify the need and to lead to a design brief.

Researching the task

This student researched information on healthy eating – using books, reports, internet and questionnaires.

Identification of a need or opportunity leading to a design brief

Since the late 1970s a number of reports have been published concerning health and diet. Since the reports have been published a percentage of people□s diets have improved slightly.
These reports include:-
~ Eating for health — DHSS 1978.
~ Proposals for nutritional guidelines for Health Education in Britain — National Advisory Committee on nutritional Education (NACNE), 1983.
~ Diet and obesity — Royal Collage of Physicians 1983.
~ Diet and cardiovascular disease — committee on medical aspects of food policy (COMA) 1984.
~ Eating for a healthier heart — British Nutrition Foundation and the Health Care Council 1985.

In the early 1990s a set of **DIETARY TARGETS** were outlined with the health of the nation.
The government set up a nutrition task force to help people in the country to eat more healthy foods.
By the year 2005 the nation should have:-
~ Reduced the average percentage of food energy derived from saturate fatty acids by at least 35% (to 11%).
~ Reduced the average percentage of food energy derived from total fat by at least 12% (to 11%).
~ Reduce the proportion of men and women aged 16—64 who are obese by at least $\frac{1}{2}$ and $\frac{1}{3}$ respectively.

To see the DRVs and EARs for the population as a whole see the charts on the following page. The concern for the nation to eat a more healthy diet is after proof from experts that eating a poor diet can have serious health effects. The links between diet and health shows that obesity is linked to energy intake; heart disease to total fat intake; dental care to sugar intake.
Nutrition education has a greater priority now because of changes in recent years e.g.: a greater range of foods particularly convenience, snack and fast foods.
Many foods often contain large amounts of fat, sugar and salts which are becoming part of most people□s diet. Nutrients such as protein, starch, vitamins, NSP and minerals should be eaten regularly and people should make sure that they do eat a variety of foods so that in particular a variety of vitamins and minerals are included in their diet.

The health of the nation have now produced a new set of guidelines for a healthy diet.
These are:-
~ Enjoy your food.
~ Eat a variety of different foods every day.
~ Eat plenty of foods rich in starch and NSP (fibre — unit 6).
~ Don□t eat too much fat.
~ Don□t eat sugary foods too often.
~ Look after the vitamins and minerals in your food.
~ If you drink alcohol keep within sensible limits.
~ Eat the right amount to be a healthy weight.

I have found some information off the Internet and I have included it as well.

The student designed a questionnaire to find out a gap in the market which they could then help in. Finally the student summarized the results of the questionnaire and produced bar charts of some of the results so they could be more easily analysed. She used a computer to produce the questionnaire and charts.

Design brief

From this research the student developed the following design brief. 'Design and make new marketable low-fat product aimed at 14–16 yr olds.'

The student attended The Lady Eleanor Holles school.

Questionnaire

As a year 10 student at The Dronfield School. I am now involved in my GCSE Food Technology Coursework, which is to design a new healthy eating product. To do this I have to research the needs of the public so that I can produce a product which would hopefully be popular and sell well:

1. Age

   0-10 ☐   11-19 ☐   20-45 ☐   46+ ☐

2. Do you eat a healthy diet?

   Yes ☐   No ☐   Don't know ☐

3. Why? _____

4. a) Do you think more healthy food products should be brought onto the market?

   Yes ☐   No ☐

   b) If yes, what type of products would you like to see on the supermarket shelf?

5. If a food manufacturer was to design a new healthy food, would you like it to be:-
   a) low in fat ☐
   b) low in sugar ☐
   c) high in fibre ☐
   You may tick more than one box.

6. Who should the product

   Children ☐
   Teenagers ☐
   Adults ☐
   Elderly ☐
   Everybody ☐

Results

Summary of results

9 people filled in my questionnaire.

Q1—Age
   0-10   1
   11-19   3
   20-45   4
   46+   1

Q2 — Do you think you eat a healthy diet?
   Yes   3   No   6   Don't know   0

Q3—Why?
   I eat too many sugary and fatty foods *(4 people)*
   I eat too many take-aways *(1 person)*
   I have chips nearly every day *(1 person)*
   I eat plenty of fruit and vegetables *(1 person)*
   I do not eat too many cakes and biscuits now *(1 person)*
   I have cut out all my chips and fried foods *(1 person)*

Q4a) Do you think more healthy food products should be brought onto the market?
   Yes   8   No   1   Don't know   0

Q4b) If yes what type of products would you like to see on the supermarket shelf?
   New savoury products, quiche, pasta products, new types of salad, healthy desserts, new pastry products.

Q5 If a food manufacturer was to design a new healthy food product would you like it to be?
   Low in fat   6   low in sugar   2   high in fibre   1

Q6 Who should the product be aimed at?
   Children   1   Teenagers   8   Adults   0
   Elderly   0   Everybody   0

Carrying out research

These two pages refer to coursework for OCR Food Technology, Internal assessment objective 2: Research into the design brief which results in a specification (12 marks).

There are several steps to carrying out research that will result in a design specification.

Examine the intended purpose, form and function of the product. Look at the task and design brief to explain the purpose of your product.

- Write questionnaires and carry out surveys to find out the needs of your target group for both the food product and the packaging (distribute a minimum of 6 and a maximum of 10 questionnaires).
- Collect information associated with packaging labelling.
- Consider HACCP (full course only).
- Evaluate existing food products (food and packaging) using a range of communication techniques against the identified needs of your target group. Include an analysis. Select 6 products giving information in design for 2 of these if you are doing the full course. For the short course select 3 products giving information in depth for 2 of them.
- Collect information on processing techniques for large-scale manufacture – look at no more than 2 commercial production methods (full course only).
- Research from a variety of sources (full course only).
- Collect other information appropriate to task.
- Analyse all the research before developing a detailed specification that shows consideration of a system to control production of the product in quantity.

Design brief

Design and make a new marketable low fat product aimed at 14–16 year olds.

This is how Internal assessment objective 2 can be carried out for this brief.

- Brainstorm to examine the purpose of the product.
- Identify low fat foods and ingredients using food tables, nutrition analysis programs and the Internet.
- Carry out a survey to find out teenagers' opinions on low-fat products, their favourite foods and the qualities they would look for. Analyse the results.
- Investigate and evaluate how existing products meet the needs of teenagers.

This student has evaluated a range of existing products against the needs identified in her questionnaire. A number of products have been evaluated by using a chart, then two of these have been evaluated in more depth.

Evaluating existing products

Name of product	Price	Tasty	Attractive	Low fat	No of portions	Type (Fresh/ Frozen/ Chilled)	Pic of prod	Packaging Strong	Packaging Easy to dispose	Packaging Attractive	Ready made meal	Snake	Between £1—2	Sold singularly
Tesco — Pizza Slices	£1.29	Yes	7/10	✘	4	Frozen	✔	✔	✔	6/10	✘	✔	✔	✘
Tesco — Cannelloni (frozen)	99p	Yes	9/10	✘	1	Frozen	✔	✔	✔	9/10	✔	✔	✘	✔
Heinz — Weight watchers Carbonara	£1.89	Average	5/10	✔	1	Frozen	✔	✔	✔	5/10	✔	✔	✔	✔
Tesco — Grill Steaks	£1.79	Yes	9/10	✘	6	Frozen	✔	✔	✔	9/10	✘	✘	✔	✘
McVities — Go Ahead caramel crisps	£1.39	Yes	9/10	✔	10	Fresh	✔	✔	✔	8/10	✔	✔	✔	✘
Jacobs — Vitalinea Choc & Orange Bar	72p	Average	6/10	✔	5	Fresh	✔	· ✘	✘	6/10	✘	✔	✘	✘

Tesco — Cannelloni (frozen):-
99p — quite a good price. A small portion but the quality looks very good. The product is decribed as "fresh pasta rolls filled with a rich tomato and beef sauce" it certainly looks worth its money. The product looks tasty and attractive, also it is described as a very traditional Italian meal. The preparation is very easy and quick if cooked in a microwave. There is also two ways to cook this product:- Microwave and oven.
This product needs to be stored in the freezer, and then re-cooked.
The packaging is quite attractive but the name of the product isn't as catchy as some products. The front of the packaging is informative, with a detailed description of the product. There is also a description of where the product originated from and an explanation of the ingredients that are in the product. The product has quite a high fat content so it is definitely not low fat. The packaging gives a lot of information about the product so the customer knows exactly what they are buying.
Overall the packaging is reasonably attractive but could do with more variety of bold colours. The product looks very appetizing and extremely tasty.

McVities — Go ahead caramel crisps:-
£1.39 (pack of 10) which is a reasonable price considering it is a low fat product. Each bar works out at about 14p. Each bar is quite small but a good snack size. The packaging states very clearly that the product is 85% fat free, but it still has a fat content of 3.2 (of which 2.0 are saturates) which is quite low. The product looks very tasty and the ingredients in the product are shown on the front of the packaging. The name "Go Ahead" is renowned for being a low fat product, and on the back of the packaging the variety of other existing products by McVities that are part of the "Go Ahead" range. The packaging is attractive and the colour is bold and eye catching. The different fonts used help to sell the product. On the back of the packaging there is all the required information on the packaging but there is also extra information about how to "Count the fat content" and also information on the McVities's range of products available on the market.
I think this product is interesting and attractive it is basic and informative. The picture of the product looks tasty and appetizing.

Other research

This could include research into:

- ways to decrease fat content
- suitability for different groups of people
- production methods
- labelling
- packaging and materials, including environmental issues
- function of ingredients
- HACCP
- British and European standards

This could result in a detailed specification that should reflect the needs identified by teenagers and the purpose of the product. However, a final specification will need to be written for the final product in Internal assessment objective 4.

Systems and control

You should consider a system to control quality. You need to make a statement within your specification to show that the product has to be made in quantity, and controls must be in place to get consistent standards. This can include controls for:

- weighing
- measuring
- preparation
- making
- cooking
- hygiene
- testing
- tasting
- packaging.

At this stage, these controls can apply to any product unless you have chosen to develop a specific product, such as biscuits. Then the control information can be clearer. Cutters and measuring sticks will help control the size and shape of many types of biscuit.

Note: A control system for the final product is not developed until Internal assessment objective 4.

Specification

My product needs to be:-

- ✔ Aimed at 14-18 year olds
- ✔ Low fat
- ✔ Tasty
- ✔ Ready made meal
- ✔ Priced between £1-£3
- ✔ Snack (quick and easy to cook)
- ✔ Fresh
- ✔ Sold singularly
- ✔ Suitable for manufacture in quantity. This means that a system needs to be designed which controls quality so that all finished products are of the same standard.

With packaging that is:-

- ✔ Bright/attractive
- ✔ Shows a picture of the product
- ✔ Shows the low fat symbol
- ✔ Easy to dispose of
- ✔ Lightweight/strong and durable

To achieve this:-

- ➢ Ingredients must be weighed and measured accurately using scales and measuring equipment etc.
- ➢ Preparation of ingredients must be consistent e.g.
- ➢ Chopping – a processor would ensure more uniformity.
- ➢ Rolling of dough – using a template to cut round ensuring that all the products are the same shape and size, using a measuring stick to check depth of dough.
- ➢ A flow chart made detailed and clear to follow, so that the product is made to the same high quality and standard every time.
- ➢ Oven temperatures and cooking times must be carefully controlled and checked regularly.
- ➢ The product must be made in hygienic conditions.
- ➢ The product should be regularly tested and evaluated.
- ➢ Packaging should be of the same quality e.g. same material, same colours and size. Printing of the label to be done by a machine and checked regularly.

This product specification is for the following design brief. Design and make a new marketable low-fat product aimed at 14–18 year olds.

Generating design proposals

p.113–14

5.1.3a–g, 5.1.11a

These two pages refer to coursework for OCR Food Technology, Internal assessment objective 3: Generate design proposals (12 marks).

You need to generate a range of design proposals and evaluate them against the design specification and decide if the ideas meet the need. You should modify them if necessary. Then choose a solution to develop further. Work should be presented using a range of graphic techniques and ICT including computer-aided design.

For the short course in Food Technology, it is suggested that no more than two appropriate proposals should be developed.

For the full course, it is suggested that six appropriate proposals should be considered (two products if they are complex). At least three people should be used to test, taste and evaluate the products.

Getting ideas

Use recipe books and magazines to give you ideas to adapt for design work. You can analyse existing products to get more information. Select the recipes that you wish to trial and show what adaptations you will make.

This work shows the results of brainstorming ideas.

Produce a plan of action

After you have brainstormed a range of design proposals, identify which ones you want to consider for further development.

Present these proposals using a range of techniques so you effectively communicate your ideas. If you are doing the full course a plan of action should now be produced so that you can consider your proposals in greater detail. Your plan of action should show planning, making and evaluating your products. Any changes to your plan of action should be shown.

Testing and evaluation

Each product should be tested on at least 3 people so that they taste and evaluate the product.

The evaluation sheet for each product should find out:

- if the product meets the design specification
- other people's views on your product
- ideas for improvement.

The final evaluation for each product should include:

- an evaluation against the specification
- whether it meets the needs – will it sell and is it cost effective?
- any problems you have had in making the product.

Example plan of action

Date	Work to be carried out at school	Work to be carried out at home	Changes I have made
Friday 1st Oct	List ingredients and equipment for Chicken and Bean Bake. Work out nutritional content.	Cost product and design evaluation sheet.	Needed to list ingredients and equipment at home for first product because school□s printer was broken.
Wednesday 6th Oct	Cook Chicken and Bean Bake.	Evaluate Chicken and Bean Bake.	
Friday 8th Oct	List ingredients and do nutritional content for Quiche Lorraine.	List equipment and cost ingredients for the Quiche Lorraine.	
Wednesday 13th Oct	Cook Quiche Lorraine.	Evaluate Quiche Lorraine.	
Friday 15th Oct	List ingredients and do nutritional content for Filo and Apricot Purses.	List equipment and cost ingredients for the Filo and Apricot Purses.	
Wednesday 20th Oct	Cook Filo and Apricot Purses.	Evaluate Filo and Apricot Purses.	
Friday 22nd Oct	List ingredients and do nutritional content for Fruity Muesli Bars.	List equipment and cost ingredients for the Fruity Muesli Bars.	
Wednesday 27th Oct	Half Term		
Friday 29th Oct	Half Term		
Wednesday 3rd Nov	Cook Fruity Muesli Bars.	Evaluate Fruity Muesli Bars.	
Friday 5th Nov	List ingredients equipment and do nutritional content for Chilli.	Cost Chilli.	
Wednesday 10th Nov	Cook Chilli.	Evaluate Chilli.	
Friday 12th Nov	List ingredients and do nutritional content for Lemon Sponge Fingers.	List equipment and cost ingredients for Lemon Sponge Fingers.	
Wednesday 17th Nov	Cook Lemon Sponge Fingers.	Evaluate Lemon Sponge Fingers.	
Friday 19th Nov	Do design proposal.	Finish design proposal.	

EVALUATING PRODUCT AGAINST MY SPECIFICATION

To evaluate my product correctly, I need to link the product back to the original design specification that I drew up in objective 2 to check that I have met the different criteria of my specification. To do this I will draw up a table containing the main points of my specification and check that my product meets the demands of it.

I have listed the different points in my specification. If I am satisfied that I have met the point with my product I shall place ticks in the 'satisfied' box. The number of ticks I place in the box depends on how satisfied I am.

✓✓✓ Very satisfied
✓✓   Fairly satisfied
✓   Just satisfied

If I feel that my product has not met a certain point then I shall place a cross in the 'unsatisfied' box.

SPECIFICATION	SATISFIED	UNSATISFIED
Dish contains pasta and is suitable for the cook-chill section of the supermarket	✓✓	
Dish contains some of the daily nutrient requirements of 5-12 year olds (especially calcium and protein)	✓✓	
Dish holds a reasonable price to meet family budgets	✓✓✓	
Dish has an appetizing appearance	✓✓	
Dish has a good texture	✓	
Dish contains a variety of flavours (not too bland or strong)		✗
Dish comes in suitable portions	✓	
Dish is easy to heat and serve	✓✓✓	
Dish is easy to hold and eat	✓✓✓	
Dish is hygienic and safe	✓✓✓	

Evaluating a product against the specification

HEDONIC SCALES

TASTER NUMBER	APPEARANCE	TEXTURE	FLAVOUR	COMMENTS
1	5	3	4	carrots and celery were too hard. Sauce was extremely bland. Pasta was too soft.
2	4	4	3	good appearance but a little bland
3	5	4	4	looks nice but no flavour
4	5	3	4	pasta was mushy and the carrots were too crunchy. looks nice.
5	5	4	4	chicken was nice, but dish needs more flavour
TOTALS	24/25	18/25	19/25	61/75 = 81%

EVALUATION

I have learnt quite a lot from carrying out taste testing on my product. Initially, the product looked fairly appetising but on tasting it could be seen that the carrots and celery needed more cooking to soften them more and the pasta was too soft and so was maybe overcooked. It would need less cooking to make it al'dente. The pasta was also fairly flavourless and so would need more seasoning.
The overall mark gained for the product was 81% which is not bad but could certainly be improved upon.

This shows the results from a tasting test of a design proposal for a pasta dish

Product development

These two pages refer to coursework for OCR Food Technology, Internal assessment objective 4: Product development (12 marks).

For the full course, the design proposal (food product) should be developed (trialled and tested) at least twice. The third testing is for the final product in Internal assessment objective 5.

For the short course, adapt your proposals to develop a final product and give full details of the final proposal including a final product specification.

The aim is to try to improve the product continually, taking into account the views of those tasting the product during trialling and testing.

For this section of the coursework you need a plan of action, which should include:

- trialling and testing the chosen idea

- listing the ingredients and equipment for each product (you need to explain clearly the changes being made and the reasons for these changes)
- working out the nutritional content for each product
- costing each product
- making each product
- designing an evaluation sheet for testing and tasting each product
- evaluating each product against the specification
- reasons for choice of ingredients, equipment and production method for the final product
- designing a detailed product specification
- reasons for choice of packaging materials
- planning a control system for production of the food product
- commenting on how the product can be made in quantity and the implications for quantity manufacture.

Marks are awarded for planning in Internal assessment objective 5.

Packaging

- Explain the materials to be used for the packaging, giving reasons for choice. This includes external as well as internal packaging if internal packaging is appropriate to the chosen product.

Ingredients Final Choices

Because recipe variation 2 would (had the vegetables been cooked for longer) scored full marks for each of the criteria in my specification, I have chosen to use this recipe for my final manufactured product.

The table below shows this final choice of ingredients and the reasons for their inclusion.

Vegetable oil	Lubricates vegetables, stopped them from sticking to the pan and burning during frying.
75g chopped onion	Adds texture and taste
75g mushrooms	Adds texture, taste and volume
1 yellow pepper	Adds colour, texture, taste and volume
400g chopped tomatoes and herbs	Adds colour, taste, moisture
100g no-pre-cook lasagne	Adds texture and colour, separates layers
200g low-fat fromage frais	Forms bulk of topping. Bland taste contrasts with vegetables as does its whiteness.
1 size 3 egg	To help incorporate air into the topping thereby improving the texture
450g smoked haddock	Adds flavour, substance and nutritional value

The product will be low in fat therefore is suitable for some-one who follows this diet and my tasting panel think that it is attractive and tasty. Their high marking shows that it is suitable for their (the teenage) age-group. It costs 79.56 (80)p per portion which they think of as good value for money. I think that it would also be possible to give the product a home-made image. Therefore, this recipe completely fills my specification.

Trialling and testing the chosen idea

Select one idea to progress further and make any necessary modifications. For example, if you were choosing to make a pizza you could:

- use different ingredients
- use different quantities of ingredients
- create different shapes and sizes, such as folded pizzas or mini-pizzas
- use different preparation methods such as dicing the vegetables as opposed to slicing, or using a processor instead of a grater
- arrange the toppings in different ways
- use different bases – bread or scone, packet mix or ready-made.

When making changes, you should take into account the improvements people suggested for your chosen idea during generating design solutions (Internal assessment objective 3). You need to state clearly what changes have been made and why.

Product specification

- Aimed at 14 — 18 year olds.
- Low fat — contain no more than 5g of fat per 100g of the finished product.
- A savoury product based on pasta, tuna and a roux sauce.
- Contains a variety of vegetables.
- Good sensory qualities — tasty, attractive, colourful, appetizing, moist.
- A ready-made meal.
- Sold as a single portion, 450g (+15g) in weight.
- Quick and easy to cook i.e. suitable for re-heating in the oven and microwave.
- Sold as a chilled product.
- Costs no more than £1.50 when sold as an individual portion.
- Suitable to add other ingredients in order to make a range.
- Packaged in a plastic dish, suitable for re-heating in the oven and microwave.
- Plastic dish to be vacuum packed in a cellophane bag before placing in a wax coated cardboard box, so it is easy to dispose of and is lightweight, strong and durable.
- Packaging that is bright, attractive, shows a picture of the product, low fat symbol.
- Suitable to be manufactured in quantity.

Example of a final product specification

PRODUCT DEVELOPMENT – MODIFICATION NUMBER 1

In objective 3, I made a 'macaroni cheese with peppers and sweetcorn' and although it was successful, modifications that could be made to the dish were suggested and to make the product marketable I shall put some of these suggestions into practice to see if they will improve my dish.

Firstly, it was stated that my dish was not 'cheesy' enough. To make the dish 'cheesier' this time, I shall not use mild cheddar, I shall use full flavoured cheddar cheese instead. This should add more flavour.

Secondly it could be seen that not enough au gratin topping was used in my dish so the topping was not crispy enough. To modify my dish, I shall add more au gratin topping by using more breadcrumbs which I will hand make and cheese to the top of the macaroni cheese.

Finally, it was commented that broccoli may be more appealing than peppers to children and they would add more colour and texture so I shall take the peppers out of the dish and try using broccoli instead.

I would also like to experiment with different pasta shapes so I will take the shell pasta out and use 'bow pasta' instead.

MACARONI CHEESE WITH BROCCOLI AND SWEETCORN...

NAME: Macaroni cheese with broccoli and sweetcorn
DESCRIPTION: Pasta in a cheesy sauce with broccoli and sweetcorn covered in a crisp au gratin topping.

INGREDIENTS AND MODIFICATIONS:

Previous Ingredients	Modifications
100g shell pasta	→ 100g bow pasta
150g cheese (grated)	→ 150g full flavour cheese
30g margarine	
30g flour	
500ml milk	
2 tablespoons breadcrumbs	→ 4 tablespoons home-made breadcrumbs
	→ 50g broccoli
50g red pepper	
50g sweetcorn	
Salt and pepper	
Basil leaf to garnish	

NB. THIS DISH WILL SERVE TWO PEOPLE

I chose to use bow pasta instead of shell pasta because I wished to see whether this would make the dish more interesting or give it a better texture.

I used full flavour cheddar cheese instead of mild cheese because this would make the sauce cheesier and tastier as this had been stated in the hedonic scales previously.

For the final idea

- Include a system that will make sure you can control the quality of size, shape and results such as a template, a cutter, measuring equipment.
- Use HACCP.
- Give details of the final design including a final product specification.
- Present your solution using a range of graphic techniques and ICT.

This work shows the evaluation and modification of products by students

Product planning and realization

pp.117–18

5.1.5a–b, 5.1.8i

These two pages refer to coursework for OCR Food Technology, Internal assessment objective 5: Product planning and realization (52 marks).

At this stage of the coursework you will be making the final product and evaluating it against the target group and the detailed product specification. The marks for evaluation are given in Internal assessment objective 6.

Making the final product

To make the final product you need to:

- produce a flow chart to show the ingredients, equipment and order of work as a process
- include appropriate checks at each stage to ensure a quality product is made
- show how the product will meet quality standards
- use appropriate skills and techniques for the task
- weigh, measure and work economically and accurately
- cost the final product and work out its nutritional content
- come up with a final package idea and **logo**.

What is being measured during practical work?

During all practical work for Internal assessment objectives 3, 4 and 5 you will be assessed on:

- using tools and equipment accurately, safely and effectively
- being able to overcome problems and adapt to changes
- weighing and measuring accurately and considering waste of products
- using a variety of skills, equipment and techniques
- achieving high quality work.

The assessment of practical work starts in Internal assessment objective 3 but all the marks for this section are awarded to Internal assessment objective 5.

This is an example of a flow chart for a final product.

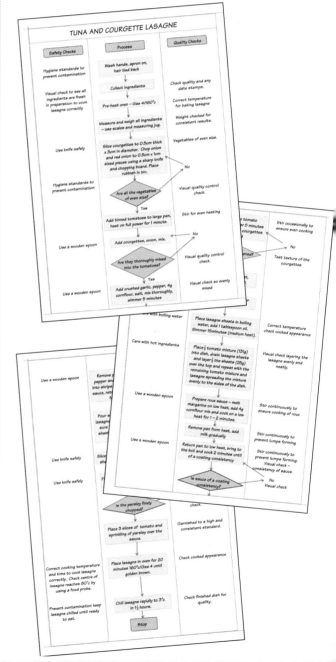

Checklist for this stage in the coursework

Have you:

- written a detailed flow chart of the process using the standard symbols shown in the specification with reference to the control systems
- provided photographic evidence of the final product
- been resourceful and adaptable with materials, food and equipment
- combined a range of skills appropriate to the task
- shown a high standard of safe working procedures
- produced a food product to a high standard
- where appropriate applied a range of industrial techniques?

Packaging for your final product

When you design your packaging for the product, you will need to decide what information is needed on the label. A labelled drawing of packaging is required. This can be drawn as a net. You can copy an existing packaging net if it is the correct size and shape. The net should be drawn to scale. You can also draw and label the internal packaging if this is appropriate for the food product.

Packaging can be drawn by hand but you can use drawing packages on the computer to help produce your package if the resources are available. Both suggestions are acceptable for coursework.

If you are using a computer and have access to a scanner, you can scan in information and pictures and place them on your final packaging idea.

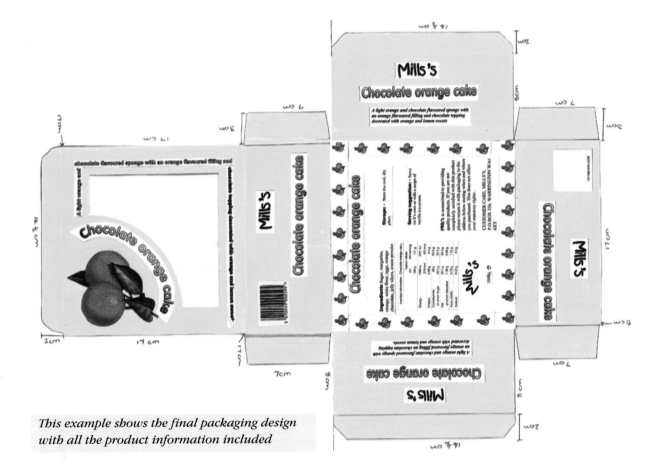

This example shows the final packaging design with all the product information included

Evaluation and testing

TRF p.119–20

5.1.11a–e

This page refers to coursework for OCR Food Technology, Internal assessment objective 6: Evaluation and testing (8 marks). In your overall coursework 5 marks are available for overall presentation.

- Evaluate the product against the original task, design brief and specification. How have you met your specification? Is your product of suitable quality for the intended user?

- Decide if time, ingredients, equipment and production methods have been used appropriately.

- Did you make changes in your plans? If so, why?

- Describe how you might have done things in a better order.

- Were you able to follow your flow chart or did you need to add more detail?

- What equipment did you use and why? Could you improve on the choice of equipment?

- Analyse the performance of the control system in the manufacture of the product. Did the control checks work well?

- Did you ask sufficient questions in the final evaluation to find out if the product would be successful? How did you manage to check for quality as you worked?

- Suggest proposals for further developments, modification or improvement of food and packaging design. Give reasons to show how your final product could be improved or developed further.

- Collect people's opinions of your product and find out if they will buy it.

- Show evidence of detailed testing and tasting of the product by using a tasting group of at least three intended users. These people should be from your target group.

- Show whether your product meets the specification both for food and packaging.

- Include a photo of the final product.

This star profile is part of the evaluation of a final product.

EVALUATION OF MY SENSORY ANALYSIS...

Having completed my final sensory analysis, I am happy that my product is marketable and suitable for sale in a supermarket. I believe that my product will be popular with members of my target group and therefore will sell well.

The children that completed my sensory analysis enjoyed the product. The results are encouraging. They show that the dish was tasty and appealing. The au gratin topping was crunchy contrasting with the cheesy sauce. The broccoli was well cooked and the bacon quite crispy. The dish was interesting enough so no more ingredients need to be added. The children also confirmed that the pasta was al dente.

The parents of the children completing the sensory analysis were also happy about the dish and were especially pleased with the nutritional content of the dish as the lack of nutrients had put them off buying cook - chilled products in the past.

My product therefore meets the criteria of my specification in these factors.

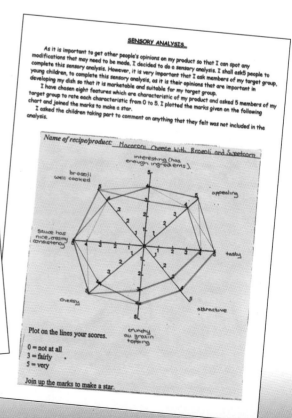

SENSORY ANALYSIS

As it is important to get other people's opinions on my product so that I can spot any modifications that may need to be made, I decided to do a sensory analysis. I shall ask 5 people to complete this sensory analysis. However, it is very important that I ask members of my target group, young children, to complete this sensory analysis, as it is their opinions that are important in developing my dish so that it is marketable and suitable for my target group.

I have chosen eight features which are characteristic of my product and asked 5 members of my target group to rate each characteristic from 0 to 5. I plotted the marks given on the following chart and joined the marks to make a star.

I asked the children taking part to comment on anything that they felt was not included in the analysis.

Name of recipe/product: Macaroni Cheese with Broccoli and Sweetcorn

interesting (has enough ingredients)

broccoli well cooked

appealing

Sauce has nice, creamy consistency

tasty

cheesy

attractive

crunchy au gratin topping

Plot on the lines your scores.

0 = not at all
3 = fairly
5 = very

Join up the marks to make a star.

ADDRESSES AND RESOURCES

Books and resources

British Nutrition Foundation, High Holborn House, 52–54 High Holborn, London WC1V 6RQ. Information resources, packs, videos, data sheets and a valuable Internet site (see page 143).

Campden and Chorleywood Food Research Association, Chipping Campden, Gloucestershire GL55 6LD. Produces technical papers and guidelines for the food industry. Up-to-date information on food, including *Product Development Guide for the Food Industry* – a book on industrial practice.

Causeway Press – *GCSE Design and Technology: Food Technology,* Barker, Kimmings, Phillips.

Collins Real World Technology – *Food Technology,* Inglis, Plews, Chapman.

DATA, 16 Wellesbourne House, Walton Road, Wellesbourne, CV35 9JB. *Food Technology in Practice.* This resource provides secondary teachers with materials to help them plan the curriculum more effectively and introduces important aspects of knowledge and skill that underpin work in Food Technology. The resource has a strong focus on industrial practice and the use of information technology.

Heinemann Educational
Examining Food and Nutrition, Jenny Ridgwell, 1996
Examining Food Technology, Anne Barnett, 1996
Skills in Food Technology, Jenny Ridgwell, 1997
Understanding Ingredients, Anne Barnett, 1998

Heinemann Library – *Food in Focus.* A series of books based on food products.

HMSO
The Composition of Foods, McCance and Widdowson.
Food Portion Sizes, MAFF, second edition, 1994. A very useful book to refer to for the average size of food ingredients.

Meat and Livestock Commission, Winterhill House, Snowdon Drive, Milton Keynes MK6 1AX. A series of educational resources to support Food Technology.

National Dairy Council, 5–7 John Princes St, London W1M OAP. Information on nutrition and current issues.

Nuffield Design and Technology Project, Longman Education. A range of materials for key stages 3 and 4.

Oxford University Press – *Food Technology at GCSE,* Anita Tull.

Ridgwell Press – *Tasting and Testing, Nutrition and Food Design, Food Coursework, Food Activities, Food Temperature Control, Food Systems and Control, Food Product Development, Food Technology Glossary.*

Stanley Thornes – *Design and Make It: Food Technology.* Books produced by in conjunction with NEAB to support Food Technology along with a video linked to a Channel 4 TV series.

Which? Ltd., 2 Marylebone Road, London NW1 4DF. *Which?* reports and useful tasting and evaluation information.

Videos, computer programs, CD-ROMs, resources

Classroom Video, Darby House, Bletchingley Road, Merstham, Redhill, Surrey, RH1 3DN. Videos on food preservation, flour, bread and baking, biscuit making, and meat processing.

DATA, 16 Wellesbourne House, Walton Road, Wellesbourne, CV35 9JB.
The Food Story. A video telling the story of the development of a range of vegetarian sausages.

Economatics – *HACCP Software.* Gives students an insight into HACCP and how it is used in industry. Available from Economatics Education Ltd, Epic House, Darnall Road, Attercliffe, Sheffield S9 5AA.

Fish Bytes (PC version). The Sea Fish Industry Authority, 18 Logie Green Road, Edinburgh, EH7 4HG.

Hampshire Microtechnology Centre, Connaught Lane, Portsmouth PO6 4SJ. Computer programs which include *Nutrients* and *Diet Analysis.*

Heinemann Educational Publishers, Halley Court, Jordan Hill, Oxford, OX2 8EJ *ICT Activities for Food Technology* – resource pack with CD-ROM.

Meat and Livestock Commission, Winterhill House, Snowdon Drive, Milton Keynes MK6 1AX. *The Meat in Your Sandwich.* Video about sandwich design – free.

Ridgwell Press, PO Box 3425, London SW19 4AX.
Risk Assessment – a video on the risks in food preparation – available from Ridgwell Press.
Food in Focus – a CD-ROM on nutritional analysis – available from Ridgwell Press.
ICT and Food Technology – resource pack with CD-ROMs *New Foods CD-ROM*

TEP – *GCSE Understanding Design and Technology,* Food Technology CD-ROM. Available from Quaternary Education Ltd., The Deer House, Dunstall Road, Barton-under-Needwood, Staffs DE13 7BR.

GLOSSARY

added value a food product with something added to please the consumer which increases its cost. For example, chopping up carrots so that they are ready prepared for a stir-fry, which makes the meal quicker to prepare

additives substances added to foods in small amounts to perform a function such as to preserve, colour or flavour a product

ambient temperature normal room temperature (20–25°C)

analytical testing testing for the number of micro-organisms in a sample of the product

blanching the term blanch means 'to whiten'. Vegetables are blanched by dipping them into boiling water before freezing them to destroy enzymes which cause the food to change colour and deteriorate.

blast chill to cool food quickly by blasting it with cold air

blast freezing quick freezing that makes small ice crystals which do less damage to the food than slow freezing

brand a particular make of product, usually with a well-known name (e.g. Heinz baked beans)

CAD computer-aided design (e.g. programs used for designing packaging)

CAM computer-aided manufacture (e.g. using a computer to help control baking temperatures)

component a part of something (e.g. pastry is a component of apple pie)

concept screening looking at lots of ideas and choosing the most suitable

cook-chill food that has been cooked, fast chilled and then stored at low temperatures

cook-freeze food that has been cooked, fast frozen and then stored below freezing point

critical control point (CCP) a point in the production process that is essential to control for safety

cross-contamination the transfer of a hazardous substance, such as bacteria, from one area to another

danger zone the temperature range in which bacteria thrive (5–63°C)

database a set of data held on a computer (e.g. nutrition information)

diet the food and drink that we eat

Dietary Reference Values (DRVs) DRVs show the amount of food energy or other nutrients needed by people of different ages

due diligence in food preparation this means that the company has set up systems to help avoid contamination of food products

e mark the big e beside the weight of a product means that the average quantity must be accurate

E numbers the number given to an additive to show that it has been approved by the EU

feedback used by control systems to see if the output is correct

formulation the recipe for the product with the exact amount of ingredients required

HACCP hazard analysis and critical control point

hazard anything that can cause harm to the consumer

high-risk area the section in the food preparation area where food is most likely to be contaminated by bacteria

high-risk foods those most likely to encourage bacterial growth

image board a display of pictures and drawings to give ideas about a target group or a range of products

key words important words that may relate to the design brief

logo the symbol of a company used on products

low-risk area section in the food preparation area where food is less likely to be contaminated by bacteria

macronutrients protein, fat, carbohydrate

MAP modified atmosphere packaging

marketable product one that appeals to people and will sell when it reaches the shops; to succeed, all products must be marketable

micronutrients vitamins and minerals

modelling to experiment with an idea without actually carrying it out – you can model the nutritional value of a food product

modified starch sometimes known as a smart material. It has been changed (modified) by chemically altering its properties for use in food products.

portion a portion for one is the amount of food that satisfies the needs of one person

product specification the exact details needed to make the product

quality assurance a system that is set up before a product is made and which lays down procedures for making a safe, quality product

quality control the steps in the process of making a product to make sure that it meets the standards; faulty products are removed

sensory descriptors words that describe taste, smell, texture and flavour

shelf life how long a food product can be kept, making sure it is safe to eat and good quality

star profile mathematical model of information

system made up of input, process, output and feedback

target group the person or group of people that the product is aimed at (e.g. teenagers)

tolerance level the amount of flexibility allowed when making a product – in terms of weight, colour, size – so that it meets quality standards

trend likelihood of something happening (e.g. there is a trend for more single portions)

INDEX